Taste of Home

Halloween

TASTE OF HOME BOOKS • RDA ENTHUSIAST BRANDS, LLC • MILWAUKEE, WI

Taste of Home

© 2018 RDA Enthusiast Brands, LLC
1610 N. 2nd St., Suite 102
Milwaukee WI 53212

Visit us at **tasteofhome.com** for other
Taste of Home books and products.

International Standard Book Number:
978-1-61765-768-9
Library of Congress Control Number:
2018935815

Cover Photographer: Jim Wieland
Set Stylist: Pam Stasney
Food Stylist: Sue Draheim

Pictured on front cover:
Candy Corn Conversation Cookies, page 85
Cake Eyeballs, page 86
Choco Owls, page 86
Dancing Mummies, page 87
Black & White Spider Cookies, page 89

Pictured on spine:
Brownie Spiders, page 77

Pictured on title page:
So-Easy-It's-Spooky Bat Cake, page 114

Pictured on back cover (from left):
Spooky Joes, page 45
Crescent Roll Witch Hats, page 16
Mini Pumpkin Cakes, page 174

Printed in China.
3 5 7 9 10 8 6 4 2

**Candy Corn
Quesadillas,**
page 73

GET SOCIAL WITH US

To find a recipe tasteofhome.com
To submit a recipe tasteofhome.com/submit
To find out about other *Taste of Home* products shoptasteofhome.com

 LIKE US
facebook.com/tasteofhome

 TWEET US
twitter.com/tasteofhome

 FOLLOW US
@tasteofhome

 PIN US
pinterest.com/taste_of_home

TABLE OF CONTENTS

Hot Dog Mummies with Honey Mustard Dip, page 7
Day of the Dead Cookies, page 187

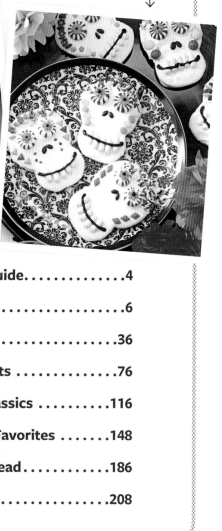

PUMPKIN
CARVING GUIDE
Grab a few tools, follow these helpful tips and get started carving spooktacular jack-o'-lanterns.

THE BASIC CARVING TOOL KIT
You can buy a pumpkin carving kit at any big-box store. Add a few household items and you're all set.

Painter's tape to hold a template

Big spoon or ice cream scoop to remove pulp

Carving kit includes mini saw, mini awl and pumpkin scraper

Pushpins or mini awl to transfer a design from template to pumpkin

Carving saw or steak knife to make precise cuts

Putty knife or scraper to thin inner walls of pumpkin

Drill bits to make patterns

Linoleum cutter to etch designs into pumpkin without carving all the way through

HOW TO CARVE YOUR PUMPKIN

No matter how simple or complex the design, each jack-o'-lantern starts out the same way. Follow these steps to carve a beauty.

1. Cut a Hole Mark a circle using a paper plate as a guide. Cut with a mini saw or serrated knife. Angle the edge slightly to create a ledge for the lid. Remove pulp from lid bottom.

2. Scoop Out Inside Use a big spoon or ice cream scoop to remove seeds and pulp. Save the seeds for roasting (see page 177). Use a putty knife or scraper to shave down flesh from interior walls for easier carving.

3. Apply Template Position a design template on the pumpkin; secure it with painter's tape. Use pushpins or a mini awl to trace the outlines as a carving guide.

4. Carve Work slowly, following the dotted outlines of the design. Use a mini saw to maneuver around curves and into tight angles.

LIGHT 'EM UP!

Although traditional votives do the trick, here are some safer, longer-lasting light sources.

Glow sticks vary in size and light intensity. A few small sticks give your gourd a soft blush; bigger, brighter sticks make it shine.

Battery-operated candles look like traditional candles, and they're not a fire hazard.

Holiday lights glow from the inside out. Or, for a quick display, wrap a whole pumpkin with a string of lights.

Special LED light kits for Halloween can mimic a flickering candle or change colors for dazzling effects. Push lights designed for closets and hallways also work.

CREEPY
BITES & SIPS

HOT DOG MUMMIES WITH HONEY MUSTARD DIP

These flaky mummy bites are instant party hits! The accompanying mustard dip adds just the right kick.

—JESSIE SARRAZIN LIVINGSTON, MT

PREP: 25 MIN. • **BAKE:** 10 MIN.
MAKES: 20 APPETIZERS (ABOUT 1 CUP DIP)

- 1 **tube (8 ounces) refrigerated crescent rolls**
- 20 **miniature hot dogs**
- 1 **large egg**
- 2 **teaspoons water**
  Dijon mustard

DIP
- ½ **cup mayonnaise**
- 3 **tablespoons Dijon mustard**
- 3 **tablespoons honey**
- 1 **tablespoon cider vinegar**
  Dash hot pepper sauce

1. Separate crescent roll dough into two rectangles; seal the seams and perforations. Cut each rectangle horizontally into 10 strips. Wrap one strip around each hot dog.

2. Place 1 in. apart on an ungreased baking sheet. In a bowl, whisk egg and water; brush over tops. Bake at 375° for 10-15 minutes or until golden brown. Using mustard, add the eyes. In a small bowl, combine dip ingredients; serve with the mummies.

GOURD-GEOUS HALLOWEEN NACHOS

My family loves nachos so much that I sometimes serve them for lunch. To get in the Halloween spirit, I used a pumpkin cookie cutter to cut out chips from pita bread. You can change the cutter shape to match any theme.

—KIM VAN DUNK CALDWELL, NJ

PREP: 40 MIN. • **BROIL:** 5 MIN.
MAKES: 10 SERVINGS

- 8 **whole wheat pita breads (6 inches)**
- ¼ **cup plus ½ teaspoon olive oil, divided**
- ¼ **teaspoon garlic salt**
- ¼ **teaspoon pepper**
- ½ **cup canned black beans, rinsed and drained**
- ⅛ **teaspoon salt**
- 2 **cups finely shredded cheddar cheese**
- ½ **cup crumbled cooked bacon**
- 4 **green onions, thinly sliced**

1. Preheat oven to 350°. Cut pita breads with a 2½-in. pumpkin-shaped cookie cutter; brush both sides with ¼ cup oil. Place on two ungreased 15x10x1-in. baking pans; sprinkle with garlic salt and pepper. Bake chips for 15-20 minutes or until toasted, stirring once halfway through baking.
2. Preheat broiler. In a small bowl, toss beans with salt and remaining oil. Layer pita chips with cheese, bean mixture, bacon and onions. Broil 3-4 in. from heat for 2-3 minutes or until cheese is melted. Serve immediately.

VAMPIRE KILLER

If you're going to hang with vampires, you're going to need a strong drink. A little garlic helps, too!

—*TASTE OF HOME* TEST KITCHEN

PREP: 5 MIN. + STANDING
MAKES: 8 SERVINGS

- 1 **serrano pepper, seeded and quartered**
- 2 **garlic cloves, crushed**
- 1 **lemon peel strip (2 inches)**
- 1½ **cups vodka**
  Ice

GARNISH
  Pickled baby beets

1. Place the pepper, garlic, lemon peel and vodka in a large glass or plastic container. Cover and let stand at room temperature for 1 week.

2. For each serving, fill a shaker three-fourths full with ice. Add 1½ ounces infused vodka to shaker; cover and shake for 10-15 seconds or until condensation forms on outside of shaker. Strain into a chilled martini glass. Garnish with a beet.

NOTES

WITCH'S CAVIAR

I like to serve this dip with triangle-shaped tortilla chips because they look like pointy witch hats.

—DARLENE BRENDEN SALEM, OR

PREP: 10 MIN. + CHILLING
MAKES: 4 CUPS

- 2 cans (4¼ ounces each) chopped ripe olives, undrained
- 2 cans (4 ounces each) chopped green chilies, undrained
- 2 medium tomatoes, seeded and chopped
- 3 green onions, chopped
- 2 garlic cloves, minced
- 1 tablespoon red wine vinegar
- 1 tablespoon olive oil
- ½ teaspoon pepper
  Dash seasoned salt
  Tortilla chips

In a large bowl, combine the first nine ingredients. Cover and refrigerate overnight. Serve with tortilla chips.

SKULL DEVILED EGGS

Thrill partygoers with these bone-chilling deviled eggs. The mayonnaise-filled bites are one of my favorite apps, so I had fun creating a Halloween version.

—NICK IVERSON DENVER, CO

START TO FINISH: 25 MIN.
MAKES: 2 DOZEN

- 12 **hard-boiled large eggs**
- ¼ **cup mayonnaise**
- ¼ **cup roasted sweet red pepper strips, finely chopped**
- 2 **teaspoons Dijon mustard**
- 2 **teaspoons cider vinegar**
- 1 **teaspoon paprika**
- ¼ **teaspoon salt**
- ¼ **teaspoon pepper**
- 1 **cup finely crushed corn chips**
  Whole corn chips, optional

1. Cut eggs lengthwise in half. Remove yolks, reserving whites. In a small bowl, mash yolks. Stir in mayonnaise, peppers, mustard, vinegar, paprika, salt and pepper until mixture is blended.

2. Using a small and a large straw, decorate each egg white to make a skull with eyes, a nose and a mouth. Spoon or pipe yolk mixture into egg whites. Place the crushed chips in a shallow bowl. Dip each exposed yolk into chips. Refrigerate, covered, until serving. If desired, garnish plate with corn chips.

TEST KITCHEN TIPS

- *This zippy filling hits all the right notes, but your favorite deviled egg recipe will also work with this technique.*
- *Feel free to nestle these into any chips you love.*
- *To keep calories and carbs in check, substitute Greek yogurt for the mayonnaise and serve eggs on a bed of shredded carrots.*

CRESCENT ROLL WITCH HATS

START TO FINISH: 25 MIN.
MAKES: 16 ROLLS

- **2 tubes (8 ounces each) refrigerated crescent rolls**
- **¼ cup butter, softened**
- **¼ cup minced fresh basil**
- **2 tablespoons oil-packed sun-dried tomatoes, patted dry and finely chopped**
- **½ teaspoon garlic powder**

1. Preheat oven to 375°. Unroll each tube of crescent dough; separate each dough into eight triangles. In a small bowl, mix the remaining ingredients. Spread 1 teaspoon filling along the wide end of each triangle; carefully roll up once to form brim of hat.

2. Place 2 in. apart on ungreased baking sheets. Bake 10-12 minutes or until golden brown. Rotate halfway through baking to ensure even browning.

It doesn't take magic to transform these crescent rolls into charming witch hats—just a few minutes and a couple of ingredients. They're so good, you'll want to make a double batch.

—MARA FLETCHER BATESVILLE, IN

GRUESOME GREEK DIP

Guests will help themselves to seconds of this savory dip. The orange color makes it fitting for a Halloween party.

—GINA WILSON AUSTIN, TX

START TO FINISH: 20 MIN.
MAKES: 2½ CUPS

- 1 **can (4 ounces) small shrimp, rinsed and drained**
- 3 **tablespoons lemon juice, divided**
- 1 **teaspoon Greek seasoning**
- 1 **package (8 ounces) cream cheese, cubed**
- ¾ **cup crumbled feta cheese**
- ½ **cup chopped roasted sweet red peppers, drained**
- 1 **garlic clove, peeled**
- 1 **tablespoon minced fresh parsley Baked pita chips**

1. In a small bowl, combine the shrimp, 1 tablespoon lemon juice and Greek seasoning; set aside.

2. In a food processor, combine the cream and feta cheeses, red peppers, garlic and remaining lemon juice; cover and process until smooth. Stir into the shrimp mixture.

3. Transfer to a serving bowl. Cover and refrigerate until serving. Just before serving, stir the dip and garnish with parsley. Serve with pita chips.

NOTES

SKEWERED EYEBALLS

These stuffed mushrooms are awfully tasty. The sword picks may look threatening, but they help folks grab their share of the finger food.

—MATTHEW HASS FRANKLIN, WI

PREP: 25 MIN. • **BAKE:** 10 MIN.
MAKES: 2 DOZEN

- 24 **medium fresh mushrooms (about 16 ounces), stems removed**
- 10 **bacon strips, finely chopped**
- ½ **cup finely chopped red onion**
- 2 **garlic cloves, minced**
- 2 **teaspoons minced fresh basil**
- ½ **teaspoon minced fresh thyme**
- 1 **container (8 ounces) cherry-size fresh mozzarella cheese**
- 24 **ripe olive slices**
- 24 **orange sword picks or toothpicks**

1. Preheat oven to 400°. Place mushroom caps in an ungreased 15x10x1-in. baking pan. In a large skillet, cook bacon over medium heat until crisp, stirring occasionally. Remove with a slotted spoon; drain on paper towels. Discard drippings, reserving 2 teaspoons in pan.

2. Add onion to drippings; cook and stir over medium heat 2-3 minutes or until tender. Add garlic, basil and thyme; cook 1 minute longer. Remove from heat; stir in the bacon.

3. Place about 1 teaspoon bacon mixture into each mushroom cap. Bake 7-9 minutes or until tender. Top each mushroom with a cheese ball; bake 3-4 minutes longer or until cheese is softened. Remove from oven; immediately press an olive slice on top of cheese. Insert a sword pick into each cheese ball. Serve warm.

MAGIC POTION PUNCH

At a Halloween party, the more creepy the food, the better! I like to make a decorative ice ring when I serve this great green punch.

—MICHELLE THOMAS BANGOR, ME

START TO FINISH: 10 MIN.
MAKES: ABOUT 4 QUARTS

- 2 **packages (3 ounces each) lime gelatin**
- ½ **cup sugar**
- 1 **cup boiling water**
- 3 **cups cold water**
- 1 **quart non-carbonated lemon-lime drink, chilled**
- 1½ **quarts lemon-lime soda, chilled**

Dissolve gelatin and sugar in boiling water; add cold water. Transfer to a punch bowl. Stir in lemon-lime drink and soda.

GUMMY WORM ICE RING *To keep Magic Potion Punch cold during your party, chill it with a gummy worm ice ring. Here's how: Fill a ring mold halfway with water. Freeze until solid. Top with gummy worms; add enough water to almost cover. Freeze until solid. To unmold, wrap bottom of the ring with a hot, damp dishcloth. Turn out onto a baking sheet; place in a punch bowl.*

MUMMY-WRAPPED BRIE

You can assemble our baked Brie appetizer in advance and bake it right before the party.
—*TASTE OF HOME* TEST KITCHEN

START TO FINISH: 30 MIN.
MAKES: 10 SERVINGS

- 1 **package (17.3 ounces) frozen puff pastry, thawed**
- ¼ **cup apricot jam**
- 1 **round (16 ounces) Brie cheese**
- 1 **large egg**
- 1 **tablespoon water**
  Apple slices
- 2 **dried cranberries or raisins**

1. Preheat oven to 400°. Unfold one sheet of puff pastry. On a lightly floured surface, roll pastry into a 14-in. square. Cut off corners to make a circle. Spread jam into a 4½-in. circle in center of pastry. Place Brie on top; fold pastry over cheese, trimming as necessary, and pinch edges to seal. Beat egg and water; brush over pastry.

2. Place on an ungreased baking sheet, seam side down. Roll remaining pastry into a 14-in. square. Cut four 1-in. strips; cut strips in half crosswise. Wrap strips around Brie, trimming as necessary. Discard the scraps. Bake for 10 minutes; brush again with egg wash. Bake until golden brown, 10-15 minutes more. For eyes, cut two circles from apple slices; place on top of Brie. Top each circle with a dried cranberry. Serve warm with apple slices.

TEST KITCHEN TIPS

- *Brush apple slices with a bit of lemon juice to keep them bright white.*
- *Use any jam or preserves in place of apricot. We like this with jalapeno or smoky bacon jam.*
- *Secure pastry strips under the Brie so they stay put. Check midway through baking: If any have sprung free, tuck them back under, then finish baking.*
- *To make this recipe year-round, skip the mummification and simply wrap cheese in one layer of puff pastry. Brush with egg wash and bake.*

CHAMPAGNE BLOOD SHOTS

There's no reason the adults can't get in on Halloween fun, too! You can make the simple syrup and chill the champagne and gelatin mixture in advance, so you'll have time for other party prep work.

—*TASTE OF HOME* TEST KITCHEN

PREP: 30 MIN. + CHILLING
MAKES: 18 SERVINGS

- ¾ cup sugar, divided
- ¼ cup water
- ¼ cup sliced fresh gingerroot
- 2 envelopes unflavored gelatin
- 1½ cups cold water
- 1½ cups chilled champagne
- 2 cups fresh strawberries, hulled and quartered
  Red food coloring, optional

1. In a small saucepan, combine ¼ cup sugar, water and ginger. Bring to a boil. Reduce heat; simmer, uncovered, 3-5 minutes or until sugar is dissolved, stirring occasionally. Remove from heat; cool to room temperature. Drain and discard ginger.

2. In a small saucepan, sprinkle gelatin over cold water; let stand 1 minute. Heat and stir over low heat until gelatin is completely dissolved. Stir in remaining sugar; cook and stir until sugar is dissolved. Remove from heat; stir in champagne. Pour into eighteen 2-oz. tall shot glasses. Refrigerate until partially set, about 25 minutes.

3. Meanwhile, place strawberries in a food processor; process until blended. Transfer to a small bowl; stir in 2 tablespoons cooled simple syrup (discard or save remaining syrup for another use). Tint red if desired.

4. To form blood in gelatin, fill a clean eye dropper with strawberry mixture. Insert into partially set gelatin and squeeze to release strawberry mixture while pulling dropper upward. Refrigerate until firm.

SILLY SNAKE SUB

This slithering sub makes a fun and tasty centerpiece. Add your own zany, creative touches and feel free to mix and match the meat and cheeses to suit your family's tastes. And if you want the sub to look like a centipede, you also can add breadsticks or pretzel rods to make legs.

—LINDA OVERMAN WICHITA, KS

PREP: 15 MIN. + RISING • **BAKE:** 15 MIN. + COOLING
MAKES: 12 SERVINGS

- 12 **frozen bread dough dinner rolls**
- ¼ **cup mayonnaise**
- 10 **slices cheddar cheese, divided**
- ½ **pound thinly sliced deli turkey**
- ½ **pound thinly sliced deli ham**
- 2 **cups shredded lettuce**
- 1 **plum tomato, thinly sliced**
- ¼ **cup yellow mustard**
- 2 **pimiento-stuffed olives**
   2-inch piece thinly sliced deli ham, optional

1. Arrange rolls ½ in. apart in an S-shape on a greased baking sheet. Cover rolls with plastic wrap coated with cooking spray and let rise in a warm place until doubled, about 3 hours.

2. Preheat oven to 350°. Bake rolls 15-20 minutes or until golden brown. Cool completely on pan on a wire rack.

3. Using a serrated knife, cut the rolls crosswise in half, leaving halves intact. Spread the bun bottoms with mayonnaise. Reserve one slice of cheese; layer bottoms with remaining slices of cheese, turkey, ham, lettuce and tomato. Spread mustard over bun tops and replace tops. Using a frilly toothpick, attach an olive to front of snake for each eye. Cut reserved cheese slice into decorative shapes; place on back of snake. If desired, cut a snake tongue from ham; attach to snake. Discard toothpicks before serving.

LI'L LIPS

START TO FINISH: 20 MIN.
MAKES: 8 SERVINGS

- 1 **medium red apple**
- 1 **teaspoon lemon juice**
- ¼ **cup chunky peanut butter**
- 2 **tablespoons reduced-fat cream cheese**
- ⅛ **teaspoon ground cinnamon**
  Miniature marshmallows, optional

1. Cut apple into 16 wedges; toss with lemon juice.
2. In a small bowl, mix peanut butter, cream cheese and cinnamon until blended. Spread about 2 teaspoons of mixture onto one side of half of the apple slices; top each with a second slice, pressing lightly, to form lips. If desired, press marshmallows onto peanut butter for teeth. Refrigerate until serving.

My kids just loved helping put the marshmallow teeth between the apple slices when I made these years ago. I usually made them with red apples, but green apples would be a playful alternative.

—AGNES WARD STRATFORD, ON

SPIDER SLIDERS

We're always trying to do fun things with food to make meals memorable. Better grab one of these sandwiches before it walks away!

—FRANK MILLARD EDGERTON, WI

PREP: 20 MIN. • **BAKE:** 25 MIN.
MAKES: 12 SERVINGS

- 2 **large sweet potatoes (about 12 ounces each)**
- ½ **teaspoon salt**
- ¼ **teaspoon ground cumin**
- ¼ **teaspoon dried thyme**
- ⅛ **teaspoon ground cinnamon**
- ⅛ **teaspoon pepper**
- ¼ **cup canola oil**
- 1 **pound ground beef**
- ¼ **cup dried minced onion**
- ½ **teaspoon seasoned salt**
- 6 **slices American cheese**
- 12 **dinner rolls, split**
- 24 **pimiento-stuffed olive slices**

1. Adjust oven racks to upper-middle and lower-middle position. Preheat oven to 400°. Peel and cut sweet potatoes into ¼-in. julienne strips. Place in a greased 15x10x1-in. baking pan. Mix salt, cumin, thyme, cinnamon and pepper. Drizzle sweet potatoes with oil; sprinkle with spice mixture. Toss to coat.

2. Bake on bottom oven rack for 25-30 minutes or until golden brown and tender, turning once. Meanwhile, in a large bowl, combine beef, onion and seasoned salt, mixing lightly but thoroughly. Press onto bottom of a greased 13x9-in. baking dish. Bake on top oven rack 15-20 minutes or until a thermometer reads 160°.

3. Drain fat from baking dish; place cheese slices evenly over meat. Bake 2-3 minutes longer or until cheese is melted. Cut into 12 patties. Place one patty on each roll bottom; arrange eight fries to form spider legs. Replace tops. Press two olive slices onto cheese to form eyes.

HELPFUL HINT

Make these sandwiches
scary-fast using frozen French
fries instead of homemade
sweet potato fries.

SLITHERING HUMMUS BITES

Friends often ask me to make my hummus dip for parties. One Halloween, I decided to take it further by piping it into phyllo shells and topping it with olives and roasted red peppers to create creepy creatures.
—**AMY WHITE** MANCHESTER, CT

START TO FINISH: 20 MIN.
MAKES: 2½ DOZEN

- 1 jar (7½ ounces) roasted sweet red peppers, drained
- 1 can (15 ounces) garbanzo beans or chickpeas, rinsed and drained
- 1 garlic clove, halved
- 3 tablespoons lemon juice
- 2 tablespoons olive oil
- 2 tablespoons tahini
- ½ teaspoon salt
- 2 packages (1.9 ounces each) frozen miniature phyllo tart shells
- 30 pitted ripe olives

1. Cut one roasted pepper into 30 strips; place remaining peppers in a food processor. Add beans and garlic; pulse until chopped. Add lemon juice, oil, tahini and salt; process until the hummus is blended.
2. Pipe into shells. Stuff a strip of red pepper into each olive; press onto filled tart shells.

HALLOWEEN
SUPPERS

MINI MARTIAN BURGERS

I'm always trying to come up with fun recipes for my grandchildren. Ever since these mini burgers starred at one of their trick-or-treat parties, my grandkids have been requesting them often. They love to help make the sliders.

—PAMELA SHANK PARKERSBURG, WV

PREP: 20 MIN. • **COOK:** 20 MIN.
MAKES: 4 SERVINGS

- 1¼ **pounds ground beef**
- 1 **teaspoon salt**
- ½ **teaspoon pepper**
- 2 **cups frozen seasoned curly fries**
- 4 **slices American cheese, halved**
- 8 **Hawaiian sweet rolls, split**
- ¼ **cup pimiento-stuffed olives, drained**
  Ketchup

1. Shape ground beef into eight small patties; sprinkle with salt and pepper. In a large nonstick skillet, cook burgers over medium heat until a thermometer reads 160°, 3-4 minutes on each side. Meanwhile, bake curly fries according to package directions. When cool enough to handle, cut fries in half.

2. Add a half slice of cheese to each burger; cook until slightly melted, about 1 minute. Place burgers on rolls. Using toothpicks, attach curly fries to rolls to look like antennas and arms, and attach olives to look like eyes. Serve with ketchup.

JACK-O'-LANTERN SANDWICHES

Be prepared for happy faces when you make these eye-catching jack-o'-lanterns. We loaded the sandwiches with flavorful fillings, then made easy-to-form fun pumpkin shapes using cookie cutters.

—TASTE OF HOME TEST KITCHEN

START TO FINISH: 15 MIN.
MAKES: 8 SERVINGS

- ½ **cup mayonnaise**
- 2 **teaspoons Italian salad dressing mix**
- 16 **slices whole wheat or white bread**
- 8 **slices American cheese**
- 1 **pound shaved deli chicken or turkey**
- 8 **lettuce leaves**

1. In a bowl, combine the mayonnaise and salad dressing mix; spread over one side of each slice of bread. Top half of the slices with cheese, chicken and lettuce. Top with remaining bread.

2. Cut sandwiches with a 4-in. pumpkin-shaped cutter. Remove top slice; using a small triangular cutter and a knife, decorate as desired. Replace slice.

NOTES

_____
_____
_____
_____
_____
_____
_____
_____

CURRIED SQUASH PASTA

This stovetop supper is simple to make, and it charms my whole family of curry lovers. My kids even like it cold and ask to have it packed that way in their school lunches.

—COLETTE LOWER YORK, PA

PREP: 15 MIN. • **COOK:** 20 MIN.
MAKES: 8 SERVINGS

- 1 **pound mild bulk Italian sausage**
- 1 **tablespoon olive oil**
- 1 **medium onion, chopped**
- 1 **medium green pepper, chopped**
- 1 **large acorn squash or 6 cups butternut squash, seeded, peeled and cubed (½ in.)**
- 1 **large unpeeled apple, cubed (½ in.)**
- 2 **to 3 teaspoons curry powder**
- 1 **teaspoon salt**
- 3 **cups cooked small pasta shells**
- ¼ **cup water**

1. In a stockpot, cook and crumble sausage over medium heat until no longer pink, 5-6 minutes; remove.
2. In same pan, heat oil; cook and stir onion and pepper for 3 minutes. Add squash; cook 5 minutes. Stir in apple, curry powder and salt until vegetables are crisp-tender, 3-4 minutes.
3. Return sausage to pan; add pasta and water. Heat through.

GHOSTLY CHICKEN & PEPPER PIZZA

This friendly ghost pizza won't scare folks away from your dinner table. My whole family loves Halloween, so we like creating fun new recipes like this one. Fill it with whatever pizza toppings you like best.

—FRANCINE BOECHER QUEENSBURY, NY

PREP: 50 MIN. + MARINATING
BAKE: 10 MIN.
MAKES: 6 PIECES

- ⅔ **cup plus 2 tablespoons olive oil, divided**
- ¼ **cup lemon juice**
- 4 **garlic cloves, minced**
- 1 **tablespoon Dijon mustard**
- 2 **teaspoons dried oregano**
- ¾ **teaspoon dried thyme**
- ¾ **teaspoon pepper**
- ½ **pound boneless skinless chicken breasts**
- ¾ **cup chopped green pepper**
- ¾ **cup chopped sweet red pepper**
- 1 **loaf (1 pound) frozen pizza dough, thawed**
- 1½ **cups shredded part-skim mozzarella cheese**
- ¼ **teaspoon salt**

1. Whisk together ⅔ cup oil with next six ingredients. Reserve 3 tablespoons marinade for pizza. Add chicken to the remaining marinade; toss in a shallow dish to coat. Refrigerate, covered, 2 hours.

2. Preheat oven to 375°. Place chicken mixture in a greased 8-in. square baking dish. Bake until a thermometer reads 165°, about 22-27 minutes. When chicken is cool enough to handle, cut into bite-size pieces.

3. Meanwhile, in a small skillet, heat 1 tablespoon oil over medium heat. Cook and stir peppers until tender, 4-6 minutes. Increase oven heat to 450°.

4. Divide pizza dough in half. On a lightly floured surface, roll each half into a 12x9-in. rectangle. Transfer one rectangle to a greased baking sheet. Brush reserved marinade over rectangle to within ½ in. of edges. Top with chicken, peppers and cheese. Sprinkle with salt. Place second dough rectangle over pizza and pinch edges to seal. Using a kitchen scissors, cut out eyes and mouth. Cut bottom to form a jagged edge; pinch edges of dough to reseal. Brush with remaining oil.

5. Bake 10-15 minutes or until golden brown.

SPOOKY JOES

START TO FINISH: 20 MIN.
MAKES: 8 SERVINGS

- 2 pounds ground beef
- 2 cans (10¾ ounces each) condensed tomato soup, undiluted
- 1 teaspoon onion salt
- 2 cups (8 ounces) shredded cheddar cheese
- 8 hamburger buns, split
- 8 slices cheddar cheese

In a large skillet, cook beef over medium heat until no longer pink; drain. Stir in the soup and onion salt; heat through. Stir in shredded cheddar cheese until melted. Spoon about ½ cup onto the bottom of each bun. Cut cheese slices with 2½-in. Halloween cookie cutters; place over beef mixture. Serve bun tops on the side.

Dressing up an old favorite for the occasion, I made hearty spooky joes, served open-faced so everyone could see slices of cheese cut into Halloween shapes on top. With orange cheese curls and jack-o'-lantern Jell-O jigglers on the side, they were a hit!

—DARLA WESTER MERIDEN, IA

FLYING BAT PIZZAS

My kids love to help add the toppings and Halloween decorations on these quick and tasty Mexican-style pizzas before I put them in the oven.

—ANGELA HANKS CHARLESTON, WV

PREP: 30 MIN. • **BAKE:** 10 MIN.
MAKES: 2 PIZZAS (8 SLICES EACH)

- 1 **package (16 ounces) frozen corn, thawed**
- 1 **can (16 ounces) kidney beans, rinsed and drained**
- 1 **can (15 ounces) black beans, rinsed and drained**
- 1 **medium sweet red pepper, finely chopped**
- 1 **tablespoon chili powder**
- 1 **tablespoon cider vinegar**
- 2 **teaspoons olive oil**
- 1 **teaspoon ground cumin**
- 2 **prebaked 12-inch pizza crusts**
- 2 **cups shredded cheddar cheese**
- 2 **spinach tortillas (10 inches)**
- 1 **can (4¼ ounces) chopped ripe olives**
  Sour cream, optional

1. Preheat oven to 450°. In a large bowl, combine the first eight ingredients. Transfer half of the mixture to a food processor. Process until blended; spread over crusts. Top with remaining bean mixture; sprinkle with cheese.

2. For bats, cut three 7-in. strips from edges of each tortilla. Using kitchen shears, cut scallops along the straight edge of each strip. From each center portion, cut three bat faces. Assemble three bats on each pizza. Arrange olive pieces on bats to make eyes and mouths. Sprinkle remaining olives over pizzas.

3. Bake 10-15 minutes or until cheese is melted. If desired, serve with sour cream.

HELPFUL HINT

If you have Halloween-themed cookie cutters, use them to cut the tortillas into decorative shapes.

EYEBALL TACO SALAD

Topped with creepy peepers, this tasty taco salad is packed with beef, cheese, tomato and satisfying southwestern flavor to make everyone in your freaky family happy.

—JOLENE YOUNG UNION, IL

PREP: 45 MIN. • **BAKE:** 25 MIN.
MAKES: 10 SERVINGS

- 2½ **pounds lean ground beef (90% lean)**
- 1 **envelope taco seasoning**
- 1 **can (8 ounces) tomato sauce**
- ¾ **cup water**
- 1 **package (15½ ounces) nacho-flavored tortilla chips, crushed**
- 2 **cups shredded Monterey Jack cheese**
- 2 **cups shredded cheddar cheese**
- 4 **cups torn iceberg lettuce**
- 1 **medium red onion, finely chopped**
- 10 **slices tomato, halved**
- 1 **cup (8 ounces) sour cream**
- 10 **pitted ripe olives, halved**

1. Preheat oven to 325°. In a 6-qt. stockpot, cook and crumble beef over medium-high heat until no longer pink, 7-9 minutes. Stir in seasoning, tomato sauce and water; bring to a boil. Reduce heat; simmer, uncovered, 15 minutes, stirring occasionally.

2. Spread chips evenly in a greased 15x10x1-in. baking pan; sprinkle with Monterey Jack cheese. Top with beef mixture; sprinkle with cheddar cheese. Bake until bubbly, about 25-30 minutes.

3. Cut into ten 5x3-in. portions. Top each with lettuce and onion. Add tomatoes, sour cream and olives to make the eyeballs.

BEEF STEW WITH GHOULISH MASHED POTATOES

Guests will be delighted with the seasonal flavors of this hearty beef stew, including mushrooms and parsnips. Rich mashed potato ghosts are piped onto each bowl. You will love the convenience of prepping this in the slow cooker.

—*TASTE OF HOME* TEST KITCHEN

PREP: 30 MIN. • **COOK:** 8 HOURS
MAKES: 6 SERVINGS

- 2 **pounds beef stew meat, cut into 1-inch cubes**
- 1 **pound fresh mushrooms, halved**
- 2 **cups fresh baby carrots**
- 2 **medium parsnips, peeled, halved lengthwise and sliced**
- 2 **medium onions, chopped**
- 1½ **cups beef broth**
- 3 **tablespoons tomato paste**
- 1 **tablespoon Worcestershire sauce**
- 2 **garlic cloves, minced**
- ½ **teaspoon ground cloves**
- ¼ **teaspoon pepper**
- 8 **medium potatoes (2⅓ pounds), peeled and cubed**
- ⅔ **cup sour cream**
- 6 **tablespoons butter, cubed**
- 1 **teaspoon salt, divided**
- 1 **cup frozen peas**
- 2 **tablespoons all-purpose flour**
- 2 **tablespoons water**

1. In a 5-qt. slow cooker, combine the first 11 ingredients. Cover and cook on low for 8-9 hours or until beef and vegetables are tender.

2. About 30 minutes before serving, place potatoes in a large saucepan and cover with water. Bring to a boil. Reduce heat; cover and simmer for 15-20 minutes or until tender. Drain. Return potatoes to pan; add the sour cream, butter and ½ teaspoon salt. Mash until smooth.

3. Set aside 12 peas for garnish. Add remaining peas to the slow cooker. Increase heat to high. In a bowl, whisk flour, water and remaining salt until smooth; stir into stew. Cover and cook for 5 minutes or until thickened.

4. Divide stew among six bowls. Place mashed potatoes in large resealable plastic bag; cut a 2-in. hole in one corner. Pipe ghost potatoes onto stew; garnish with reserved peas.

HELPFUL HINT

Freeze leftover tomato paste in tablespoon-sized scoops on a plastic wrap-lined plate, then store the portions in a freezer container. Or keep a tube of tomato paste on hand. It's convenient because it keeps a long time in the fridge.

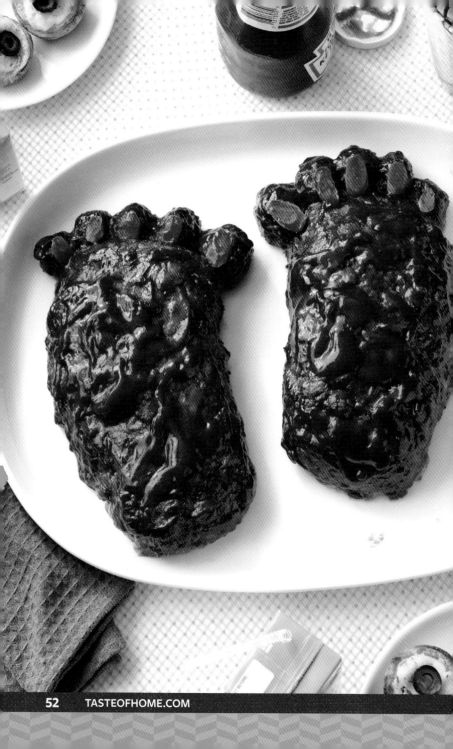

HALLOWEEN FEET LOAF

If Bigfoot pays a visit this Halloween, treat him to a larger-than-life meal. This feet loaf tastes just like your favorite home-style meat loaf. It will have enormous appeal with Sasquatch believers and doubters alike.

—SUSAN SEYMOUR VALATIE, NY

PREP: 30 MIN. • **BAKE:** 55 MIN.
MAKES: 8 SERVINGS

- 1 tablespoon canola oil
- 1 medium carrot, grated
- 1 small onion, finely chopped
- 1 celery rib, finely chopped
- ½ medium green pepper, finely chopped
- 2 cups soft bread crumbs
- 1 large egg, lightly beaten
- ½ cup 2% milk
- 1 teaspoon garlic powder
- ½ teaspoon seasoned salt
- ½ teaspoon pepper
- 2 pounds ground beef
- 1 medium carrot, cut into 10 thin slices
- ⅔ cup ketchup
- 2 tablespoons balsamic vinegar

1. Preheat oven to 350°. In a large skillet, heat oil over medium heat. Add carrot, onion, celery and green pepper; cook and stir 3-4 minutes or until tender. Cool slightly.
2. Line a 15x10x1-in. baking pan with foil; grease foil. Place bread crumbs in a large bowl. Stir in egg, milk, seasonings and carrot mixture. Add beef; mix lightly but thoroughly. Shape meat loaf mixture into two feet with indentations for toes.
3. Transfer to prepared pan. Bake the loaves, uncovered, 30 minutes. Position carrot slices on loaves for toenails. In a small bowl, mix ketchup and vinegar; brush half over meat loaves. Bake loaves for 20 minutes longer or until a thermometer reads 160°. Brush with remaining mixture; bake 5 minutes longer.

HAM & CHEESE SPIDERS

Kids really enjoy eating these creepy spider-shaped sandwiches. It's worth the effort to put them together.

—**KENDRA BARCLAY** DE KALB, IL

PREP: 30 MIN. • **BAKE:** 15 MIN.
MAKES: 5 SANDWICHES

- 1 **cup chopped fully cooked ham**
- 2 **tablespoons finely chopped onion**
- 2 **tablespoons butter, softened**
- 1½ **teaspoons prepared mustard**
- 2 **tubes (6 ounces each) small refrigerated flaky biscuits (5 count), divided**
- 1 **tube (11 ounces) refrigerated breadsticks**
- 5 **slices American cheese**
- 1 **large egg yolk**
- 1 **teaspoon water**
- 10 **ripe olive slices (about 2 tablespoons)**
- 1 **tablespoon diced pimientos**
- 1 **teaspoon poppy seeds**

1. Preheat oven to 375°. Using small pieces of foil, make forty ½-in. foil balls for shaping spider legs; coat lightly with cooking spray.

2. For filling, mix first four ingredients. On greased baking sheets, pat five biscuits into 3½-in. circles. For legs, cut each of 10 breadsticks crosswise in half; cut each piece lengthwise in half. (Reserve remaining breadsticks for another use.) Attach eight legs to each biscuit, twisting and pressing onto pan to adhere. Tuck a foil ball under the center of each leg.

3. Spoon filling over biscuits. Fold cheese slices into quarters; place over top. Pat remaining biscuits into 4-in. circles; place over cheese, pressing edges to seal.

4. Whisk together egg yolk and water; brush over tops. Attach olives for eyes; fill centers with pimientos. Sprinkle with poppy seeds.

5. Bake until golden brown, 15-20 minutes. Serve warm.

HELPFUL HINT

Don't like whole wheat pasta? Try multigrain kinds that look and taste more like white flour pasta.

SUPERNATURAL SPAGHETTI

The idea for this recipe came to me when I saw someone dip a slice of pizza into a pasta dish. My wife and kids love it and so do my friends! A quick garnish trick makes it otherworldly.

—ROBERT SMITH LAS VEGAS, NV

PREP: 20 MIN. • **COOK:** 30 MIN.
MAKES: 6 SERVINGS

- ½ **pound lean ground beef (90% lean)**
- ½ **pound Italian turkey sausage links, casings removed**
- ½ **cup chopped sweet onion**
- 4 **cans (8 ounces each) no-salt-added tomato sauce**
- 3 **ounces sliced turkey pepperoni**
- 1 **tablespoon sugar**
- ½ **teaspoon dried parsley flakes**
- ½ **teaspoon dried basil**
- 9 **ounces uncooked whole wheat spaghetti**
- 3 **tablespoons grated Parmesan cheese**
- 12 **fresh mozzarella cheese pearls**
- 12 **slices pimiento-stuffed olives**

1. In a large nonstick skillet, cook beef, sausage and onion over medium heat 6-8 minutes or until meat is no longer pink, breaking up meat into crumbles; drain.

2. Stir in the tomato sauce, pepperoni, sugar, parsley and basil. Bring to a boil. Reduce the heat; simmer, uncovered, for 20-25 minutes or until thickened. Meanwhile, cook spaghetti according to package directions.

3. Drain the spaghetti; toss with sauce. Sprinkle with Parmesan cheese. Top each spaghetti serving with two cheese pearls and two olive slices to resemble eyes.

FREEZE OPTION *Do not cook spaghetti or add to sauce. Freeze cooled beef mixture in freezer containers. To use, partially thaw in refrigerator overnight. Cook spaghetti according to package directions. Place beef mixture in a large skillet; heat through, stirring occasionally and adding a little water if necessary. Proceed as directed.*

SLITHERING SNAKE ROLL

There's nothing sinister about this snake. It's filled with meat, sweet red pepper and melted cheese. You can paint the pizza dough any color or leave it plain.
—JACLYN SCANLAN DAYTON, OH

PREP: 30 MIN. • **BAKE:** 30 MIN. + COOLING
MAKES: 12 SERVINGS

- 1 **medium sweet red pepper**
- ½ **pound fresh chorizo, casings removed, or bulk spicy pork sausage**
- ½ **pound ground beef**
- 1 **small onion, chopped**
- 2 **garlic cloves, minced**
- 1 **loaf (1 pound) frozen pizza dough, thawed**
- 2 **cups shredded Monterey Jack cheese**

FOR DECORATION
- 1 **large egg, lightly beaten**
  Green food coloring, optional
- 2 **tablespoons sesame seeds**
- 2 **slices ripe olive**

1. Preheat oven to 350°. Cut one small strip of red pepper and reserve; chop remaining pepper. In a large skillet over medium heat, cook chorizo, beef, pepper, onion and garlic, crumbling meat, until no longer pink; drain.

2. Roll dough into a 14x12-in. rectangle. Spread the beef mixture lengthwise in middle of dough; sprinkle with cheese. Wrap dough around beef-cheese mixture. Pinch seam to seal; tuck ends under. Place seam side down on a parchment-lined 15x10x1-in. baking sheet, and form into a snake shape. Whisk egg and, if desired, food coloring. Paint snake with egg wash; sprinkle with sesame seeds. Decorate with two ripe olive slices for eyes and reserved red pepper strip for a tongue.

3. Bake until edges are golden brown, 30-35 minutes. Cool 10 minutes before slicing.

MAKE-A-MONSTER PIZZA

PREP: 30 MIN. • **BAKE:** 20 MIN.
MAKES: 6 SERVINGS

- 1 tube (13.8 ounces) refrigerated pizza crust
- 1 can (8 ounces) pizza sauce
- 4 cups shredded part-skim mozzarella cheese
- 2 ounces sliced deli ham, cut into ½-in. strips
  Optional toppings: asparagus, sweet peppers, tomatoes, mushrooms, ripe olives, pineapple, pepperoni and red onion.

1. Preheat oven to 425°. Unroll pizza crust and press to fit into a greased 15x10x1-in. baking pan, pinching edges to form a rim. Bake for 8-10 minutes or until edges of crust are lightly browned.

2. Spread crust with pizza sauce; top with mozzarella cheese. Using ham strips, outline 12 sections. Arrange toppings of your choice in each section to create individual designs. Bake 10-15 minutes or until crust is golden brown and cheese is melted.

TEST KITCHEN TIP *Look to salad and olive bars for tiny treasures to boost the cuteness factor. Peppadew peppers, pickled garlic and cocktail onions are fun options. Use cookie cutters to cut sliced cheeses, meats and vegetables.*

Creepy creatures have completely taken over this Halloween meal! Since you can create a different design for each square, it's easy to cater to every diner's individual preferences.

—MARIE LOUISE LUDWIG PHOENIXVILLE, PA

YUMMY PORK MUMMY

If you're looking for the perfect main dish for your Halloween dinner party, look no further. The pork stays moist under the phyllo wrappings, and the sauce adds a Dijon zip guests won't soon forget.

—TASTE OF HOME TEST KITCHEN

PREP: 45 MIN.
BAKE: 15 MIN. + STANDING
MAKES: 4 SERVINGS

- ¾ **cup heavy whipping cream**
- ¼ **cup Dijon mustard**
- 2 **teaspoons minced fresh thyme or ½ teaspoon dried thyme**
- 1 **pork tenderloin (about 1 pound)**
- 2 **teaspoons olive oil**
- ½ **teaspoon salt**
- ½ **teaspoon pepper**
- 10 **sheets phyllo dough (14 inches x 9 inches)**
- 6 **tablespoons butter, melted**
- 1 **medium apple, peeled**

1. In a small skillet, bring cream and mustard to a boil. Reduce heat; simmer, uncovered, 10-15 minutes or until mixture is reduced to about ⅔ cup. Remove from the heat; stir in thyme.

2. Meanwhile, place the pork tenderloin on a rack in a shallow baking pan. Brush with oil; sprinkle with salt and pepper. Broil the pork 6 in. from the heat for 6 minutes. Remove from the oven; cool slightly. Change oven temperature to 400°.

3. Set aside ½ cup of mustard mixture for serving; spread the remaining mixture over the pork. Place one sheet of phyllo dough on a work surface; brush with butter. (Keep remaining phyllo dough covered with plastic wrap and a damp towel to prevent it from drying out.) Repeat layers four times. Place pork on one edge of phyllo dough; roll up tightly to form mummy's body and tuck in ends.

4. Place another sheet of phyllo dough on a work surface; brush with butter. Repeat layers three times. Cut into thin strips; wrap around pork tenderloin bundle.

5. Cut remaining sheet of phyllo dough in half; brush with remaining butter. Cut a 1-in. cube from the apple; wrap in prepared phyllo dough. Position at the wide end of bundle for a head. Save remaining apple for another use. Discard the remaining phyllo dough.

6. Place bundle in an ungreased shallow baking pan. Bake, uncovered, for 15-20 minutes or until a thermometer reads 160°. Transfer to a serving platter. Let stand for 10 minutes before slicing. Serve with reserved mustard sauce.

DRAGON LADY STEW

I love presenting this stew at Halloween. The harvest flavors and the black wild rice are perfect for the occasion. The stew tastes even better the next day.

—MARINA CASTLE KELLEY CANYON COUNTRY, CA

PREP: 25 MIN. • **COOK:** 2 HOURS
MAKES: 6 SERVINGS

- 2 **tablespoons olive oil**
- 1 **pound boneless country-style pork ribs, cubed**
- 2 **medium carrots, chopped**
- 2 **celery ribs, chopped**
- 1 **medium onion, chopped**
- 3 **garlic cloves, minced**
- 2 **bay leaves**
- 1 **tablespoon white wine**
- 1½ **teaspoons salt**
- 1 **teaspoon Chinese five-spice powder**
- ¼ **to ½ teaspoon cayenne pepper**
- ¼ **teaspoon pepper**
  Dash ground allspice or cinnamon
- 4½ **cups water, divided**
- 4 **small red potatoes, cubed**
- 1 **medium tart apple, peeled and sliced**
- 2 **tablespoons cornstarch**
  Cooked wild rice
  Chopped fresh parsley, optional

1. In a 6-qt. stockpot, heat oil over medium-high heat. Brown pork. Add carrots, celery and onion; cook and stir 2-4 minutes or until crisp-tender. Add garlic; cook 1 minute longer. Stir in the bay leaves, wine, seasonings and 4 cups water. Bring to a boil. Reduce heat; simmer, covered, until meat is tender, 1½ hours.

2. Add potatoes and apple. Cook until tender, about 15-20 minutes. Mix cornstarch and remaining water until smooth; stir into stew. Bring mixture to a boil; cook and stir until thickened, 1-2 minutes. Discard bay leaves. Serve over wild rice and, if desired, top with parsley.

FRANKENSTEIN BOO-RITOS

Chicken makes these burritos super kid-friendly, and meal-making doesn't get a lot simpler than putting them together.

—CLARA COULSON MINNEY

WASHINGTON COURT HOUSE, OH

START TO FINISH: 25 MIN.
MAKES: 8 SERVINGS

- 1 **envelope (5.6 ounces) Spanish rice and pasta mix**
- 2 **cups cubed cooked chicken**
- 1 **can (15¼ ounces) whole kernel corn, drained**
- 1 **can (14½ ounces) diced tomatoes, drained**
- 8 **spinach tortillas (10 inches)**
  Toppings: sour cream, blue corn tortilla chips, cubed and shredded cheese, ripe olives and sweet red pepper

1. In a large saucepan, prepare rice mix according to package directions. Stir in the chicken, corn and tomatoes; heat mixture through.

2. Spoon about ⅔ cup rice mixture across center of each tortilla. Fold bottom and sides of tortilla over filling and roll up. Using toppings, create a face on each burrito.

MACHETE SHREDDED BEEF SANDWICHES

Beef sirloin tip roast is the start for these tangy sandwiches. A hit of brown sugar gives the extra touch folks savor.

—*TASTE OF HOME* TEST KITCHEN

PREP: 10 MIN. • **COOK:** 8 HOURS
MAKES: 12 SERVINGS

- 1 **beef sirloin tip roast (2½ pounds)**
- ½ **teaspoon salt**
- ¼ **teaspoon pepper**
- 1 **tablespoon canola oil**
- 1 **cup each ketchup and water**
- ½ **cup chopped onion**
- ⅓ **cup packed brown sugar**
- 3 **tablespoons Worcestershire sauce**
- 2 **tablespoons lemon juice**
- 2 **tablespoons cider vinegar**
- 2 **tablespoons Dijon mustard**
- 2 **teaspoons celery seed**
- 2 **teaspoons chili powder**
- 12 **kaiser rolls, split**

1. Sprinkle roast with salt and pepper. In a nonstick skillet, brown roast in oil on all sides over medium-high heat; drain.

2. Transfer roast to a 5-qt. slow cooker. Combine the ketchup, water, onion, brown sugar, Worcestershire sauce, lemon juice, vinegar, mustard, celery seed and chili powder; pour over roast.

3. Cover and cook on low for 8-10 hours or until meat is tender. Remove meat; shred with two forks and return to slow cooker. Spoon ½ cup meat mixture onto each roll.

HAUNTED ANTIPASTO SALAD

Even a grown-up salad can be spookified. Top each serving with ghost-shaped cheese slices and all your dishes will have that haunting, festive flair.

—CYNTHIA BENT NEWARK, DE

PREP: 35 MIN.
MAKES: 12 SERVINGS

- 12 **slices provolone cheese**
- 10 **cups torn romaine**
- 2 **jars (7½ ounces each) marinated quartered artichoke hearts, drained**
- 1 **jar (8 ounces) roasted sweet red peppers, drained and julienned**
- 4 **plum tomatoes, cut into ¼-inch slices**
- 1 **small red onion, halved and thinly sliced**
- 10 **thin slices hard salami, julienned**
- 1 **can (6 ounces) pitted ripe olives, drained**
- ½ **cup Italian salad dressing**

1. Using a 4-in. ghost-shaped cutter, cut one ghost from each slice of cheese. (Reserve the remaining cheese for another use.)

2. In a large bowl, combine vegetables, salami and olives; toss to combine. Just before serving, drizzle mixture with salad dressing and toss to coat. Transfer to serving plates; top with ghosts.

CANDY CORN QUESADILLAS

Celebrate the season with a savory touch. These candy corn triangles will be a smash hit. Let kids join in the fun by using a rolling pin to crush a bag filled with nacho tortilla chips while you do the rest.

—MARIE PARKER MILWAUKEE, WI

PREP: 25 MIN. • **COOK:** 10 MIN.
MAKES: 2 DOZEN

- 1 rotisserie chicken, cut up
- 1 jar (16 ounces) salsa
- 1 cup frozen corn, thawed
- ¼ cup barbecue sauce
- ½ teaspoon ground cumin
- ½ cup butter, melted
- 8 flour tortillas (10 inches)
- 1 jar (15½ ounces) salsa con queso dip, warmed
- 4 cups shredded Mexican cheese blend
- 2⅔ cups crushed nacho-flavored tortilla chips
- ½ cup sour cream

1. In a Dutch oven, combine the first five ingredients; heat through, stirring occasionally. Brush butter over one side of each tortilla.

2. Place one tortilla in a large skillet, buttered side down. Spread with 1 cup chicken mixture; top with another tortilla, buttered side up. Cook over medium heat for 1-2 minutes or until the bottom is lightly browned. Turn the quesadilla.

3. Spread ½ cup queso dip over quesadilla; carefully sprinkle cheese along outer edge. Cook, covered, for 1-2 minutes or until cheese begins to melt.

4. Remove to a cutting board. Sprinkle crushed chips over queso dip. Cut quesadilla into six wedges. Place a small dollop of sour cream at the point of each wedge. Repeat with remaining ingredients.

STACK OF BONES

My husband devours these delicious ribs! Perfect for Halloween fun, they're prepared in a slow cooker so they turn out tender every time.
—**LINDA SOUTH** PINEVILLE, NC

PREP: 15 MIN. • **COOK:** 4 HOURS
MAKES: 4 SERVINGS

- 1 **cup chili sauce**
- 2 **green onions, chopped**
- 2 **tablespoons brown sugar**
- 2 **tablespoons balsamic vinegar**
- 1 **tablespoon Dijon mustard**
- 1 **tablespoon Worcestershire sauce**
- 1 **tablespoon soy sauce**
- 1 **teaspoon ground ginger**
- ¼ **teaspoon crushed red pepper flakes**
- ½ **teaspoon liquid smoke, optional**
- 4 **pounds pork baby back ribs**

In a large bowl, combine the first 10 ingredients. Cut ribs into individual pieces; dip into sauce. Transfer to a 5-qt. slow cooker; top with the remaining sauce. Cover and cook on low for 4-5 hours or until tender.

TRICK-OR-TREAT SWEETS

BROWNIE SPIDERS

Real spiders petrify me, but I can make an exception for these cute ones that are made from chocolate. They make perfect Halloween treats.

—ALI EBRIGHT KANSAS CITY, MO

PREP: 20 MIN. • **BAKE:** 30 MIN. + COOLING
MAKES: 9 BROWNIE SPIDERS

- 1 **package (15.8 ounces) brownie mix**
- ½ **cup semisweet chocolate chips**
- 2 **cups crispy chow mein noodles**
- 18 **candy eyeballs**

1. Prepare and bake the brownies according to package directions using an 8-in. square baking pan lined with parchment paper. Cool completely in pan on a wire rack.

2. In a microwave, melt the chocolate chips; stir them until smooth. Remove 1 tablespoon of the melted chocolate to a small bowl; reserve for attaching eyes. Add noodles to remaining chocolate; stir gently to coat. Spread onto a waxed paper-lined baking sheet, separating noodles slightly. Freeze until set.

3. Cut nine brownies with a 2¼-in. round cutter for spider bodies. Attach eyeballs using the reserved melted chocolate. With a bamboo skewer or toothpick, poke eight holes in top of each spider for inserting legs. Insert a coated noodle into each hole. Store in an airtight container.

NOTES

COLORFUL CANDIED APPLES

The glossy candy coating on these old-fashioned apples is hard, so it's best to lick them like a lollipops or cut 'em into wedges to serve. Be sure your apples are clean and dry before dipping.

—AGNES WARD STRATFORD, ON

PREP: 10 MIN. • **COOK:** 30 MIN. + STANDING
MAKES: 4 SERVINGS

- 4 **medium apples**
- 4 **wooden pop sticks or decorative lollipop sticks**
- 2 **cups sugar**
- 1 **cup water**
- ⅔ **cup light corn syrup**
- 1 **tablespoon white food coloring**
- 1 **teaspoon orange food coloring**

1. Wash and thoroughly dry apples; remove stems. Insert pop sticks into apples. Place on a waxed paper-lined baking sheet; set aside.

2. In a large heavy saucepan, combine the sugar, water and corn syrup. Cook and stir the mix over medium heat until sugar is dissolved. Stir in the food colorings. Bring to a boil. Cook, without stirring, until a candy thermometer reads 290° (soft-crack stage).

3. Remove from heat. Working quickly, dip the apples into hot sugar mixture to completely coat. Place on the prepared baking sheet and let stand until set.

WEREWOLF BROWNIES

Decorating these creatures couldn't be easier—even the kids can get in on the fun. Just make sure they don't wolf them down before the party starts!

—TASTE OF HOME TEST KITCHEN

PREP: 1 HOUR
BAKE: 25 MIN. + COOLING
MAKES: 1½ DOZEN

- ½ **cup butter, softened**
- 1 **cup sugar**
- 4 **large eggs**
- 1⅓ **cups chocolate syrup**
- 1 **teaspoon vanilla extract**
- 1 **cup all-purpose flour**
- ½ **teaspoon salt**

FROSTING

- 1 **package (3 ounces) cream cheese, softened**
- 3 **tablespoons butter, softened**
- 4 **cups confectioners' sugar**
- 3 **to 4 tablespoons 2% milk**
- 2 **ounces semisweet chocolate, melted and cooled**
- ½ **teaspoon vanilla extract**
  Red-hot candies

1. In a large bowl, cream butter and sugar until fluffy. Add the eggs, one at a time, beating well after each addition. Beat in syrup and vanilla. Add flour and salt; mix well. Pour into a greased 13x9-in. baking pan.

2. Bake at 350° for 25-30 minutes or until a toothpick inserted in the center comes out clean. Cool completely on a wire rack.

3. For frosting, in a large bowl, beat the cream cheese and butter until smooth. Gradually beat in the confectioners' sugar alternately with milk until frosting reaches desired consistency. Remove and set aside ⅓ cup of the frosting. Beat the chocolate and vanilla into the remaining frosting. Frost brownies.

4. Using a fork, make marks in the frosting to resemble hair. Cut the brownies into 18 bars. Using pastry tip #2, pipe reserved frosting for eyes and teeth. Add red-hot candies for eyes and decorate with the remaining frosting as desired to finish faces.

GHOSTLY CUSTARDS

You'll hear shrieks of delight when these not-so-spooky custards appear for dessert. These ghosts will be gobbled up in no time!

—**SUZANNE STROCSHER** BOTHELL, WA

PREP: 10 MIN. • **BAKE:** 40 MIN. + COOLING
MAKES: 8 SERVINGS

- 1 **can (15 ounces) solid-pack pumpkin**
- 1 **can (12 ounces) evaporated milk**
- ⅓ **cup sugar**
- 2 **tablespoons honey**
- 1 **teaspoon ground cinnamon**
- ¾ **teaspoon ground allspice**
- 2 **large eggs**
- 2 **cups whipped topping**
  Miniature semisweet chocolate chips

In a bowl, combine the first seven ingredients; beat on low until smooth. Place eight ungreased 4-oz. custard cups in two 8-in. square baking pans. Fill each cup with ½ cup pumpkin mixture. Pour hot water around cups into the pans to a depth of 1 in. Bake at 325° for 40-50 minutes or until a knife inserted in center comes out clean. Remove from pans to cool on wire racks. Before serving, top each with dollops of whipped topping in the shape of a ghost; add chocolate chips for eyes.

NOTES

HELPFUL HINT

You can substitute 1¾ teaspoons of pumpkin pie spice for the cinnamon and allspice this recipe calls for.

BOO!

TRICK

CANDY CORN CONVERSATION COOKIES

(pictured at left)

Add these candy corn-shaped sugar cookies to your Halloween treat platter.

—DOROTHY JENNINGS WATERLOO, IA

PREP: 45 MIN. + CHILLING
BAKE: 10 MIN./BATCH + COOLING
MAKES: 2 DOZEN

- ½ cup butter, softened
- ¾ cup sugar
- 1 large egg
- ¾ teaspoon vanilla extract
- 1¾ cups all-purpose flour
- ½ teaspoon baking powder
- ¼ teaspoon salt

ROYAL ICING

- 3¾ cups confectioners' sugar
- ⅓ cup warm water
- 4 teaspoons meringue powder
  Orange, yellow and black paste food coloring

1. In a large bowl, cream butter and sugar until light and fluffy. Beat in egg and vanilla. Combine the dry ingredients; gradually add to the creamed mixture. Divide dough in half. Shape each into a ball, then flatten into a disk. Wrap in plastic and refrigerate for 1 hour or until easy to handle.

2. On a lightly floured surface, roll one portion of the dough to ⅛-in. thickness. Cut it with a 3½-in. egg-shaped cookie cutter. Place 1 in. apart on ungreased baking sheets. Repeat with the remaining dough, cutting with 3-in. oval cookie cutter and a 1-in. triangle cookie cutter. Attach a triangle to each oval to create thought bubbles. Place on baking sheets.

3. Bake at 350° for 8-10 minutes or until lightly browned. Cool on wire racks.

4. In a small bowl, combine the confectioners' sugar, water and meringue powder; beat on low speed just until combined. Beat on high for 4 minutes or until soft peaks form. Cover frosting with damp paper towels or plastic between uses. Tint icing as desired.

5. Working quickly with one color at a time, pipe outlines on some of the cookies; fill with thinned icing. Repeat using other colors. Let dry at room temperature for several hours or until firm.

6. Add faces and writing to cookies as desired. Let stand until set. Store in an airtight container.

CAKE EYEBALLS

(*pictured at top right*)

Customize these cake balls to your liking with the flavors of your choice.

—*TASTE OF HOME* TEST KITCHEN

PREP: 1 HOUR
BAKE: 35 MIN. + FREEZING
MAKES: 4 DOZEN

- 1 package cake mix of your choice (regular size)
- 1 cup prepared frosting of your choice
- 1 package (12 ounces) each orange, pink and vibrant green Wilton candy melts
  Decorations of your choice: candy coating disks, jumbo sprinkles, candy-coated sunflower kernels, candy eyeballs, Twizzlers Rainbow Twists and Life Savers

1. Prepare and the bake cake mix according to package directions, using a greased 13x9-in. baking pan. Cool completely on a wire rack.
2. Crumble cake into a large bowl. Add frosting and mix well. Shape into 1½-in. balls. Place on baking sheets. Freeze for at least 2 hours or refrigerate for at least 3 hours or until cake balls are firm.
3. In separate bowls, heat candy melts in the microwave until melted; stir until smooth. Dip each cake ball in coating; allow excess to drip off. Decorate as desired. Let stand until set.

CHOCO OWLS

(*pictured at middle right*)

You'll have a blast making Choco Owls to add to a Halloween treat platter.

—*TASTE OF HOME* TEST KITCHEN

PREP: 1 HOUR + STANDING
MAKES: 1 DOZEN

- 1 package (10½ ounces) miniature marshmallows
- 3 tablespoons butter
- 6 cups Cocoa Krispies
- 12 wooden pop sticks
- 2 cups (12 ounces each) milk chocolate chips
- 2 teaspoons shortening
  Decorations of your choice: chocolate jimmies, halved miniature pretzels, candy corn, candy coating disks, Life Savers and Reese's pieces

1. In a large saucepan, combine the marshmallows and butter. Cook and stir over medium-low heat until melted. Stir in the cereal. Press into greased 13x9-in. pan. Allow to cool completely.
2. Using a 2½-in. round cookie cutter, cut out 12 circles. Insert a lollipop stick into each cutout.
3. In a microwave, melt chocolate chips and shortening; stir until smooth. Dip pops into chocolate; allow excess to drip off. Place on waxed paper.
4. Sprinkle with jimmies and add pretzels for ears. Add candy corn noses and use remaining candies as desired for eyes. Let stand until set.

DANCING MUMMIES

(pictured at bottom right)

Use a gingerbread boy cookie cutter to make these Halloween mummy cookies.

—DORE MERRICK GRABSKI UTICA, NY

PREP: 15 MIN. + CHILLING
BAKE: 10 MIN./BATCH + COOLING
MAKES: 3 DOZEN

- ⅔ **cup shortening**
- ½ **cup sugar**
- ½ **cup molasses**
- 1 **large egg**
- 3 **cups all-purpose flour**
- 1 **teaspoon baking soda**
- 1 **teaspoon each ground cinnamon, ginger and cloves**
- ½ **teaspoon salt**
- ½ **teaspoon ground nutmeg**
- 1 **can (16 ounces) vanilla frosting**
  Candy buttons and black decorating gel

1. In a large bowl, cream shortening and sugar until light and fluffy. Beat in the egg. Beat in the molasses. Combine the flour, baking soda, cinnamon, ginger, cloves, salt and nutmeg; gradually add to creamed mixture and mix well. Divide dough in half. Refrigerate for at least 1 hour.

2. Preheat oven to 350°. On a lightly floured surface, roll out each portion of dough to ⅛-in. thickness. Cut with a floured 3-in. dancing gingerbread boy-shaped cookie cutter. Place 2 in. apart on greased baking sheets. Bake 8-10 minutes or until edges are firm. Cool on wire racks.

3. For mummy bandages, pipe frosting using basket weave pastry tip #47. Add candy buttons and decorating gel for eyes.

BLACK & WHITE SPIDER COOKIES

Those eight-legged creatures aren't so creepy when you turn them into cookies. Make these treats any time of the year.

—*TASTE OF HOME* TEST KITCHEN

PREP: 45 MIN.
BAKE: 10 MIN./BATCH + STANDING
MAKES: 2½ DOZEN

1 package yellow cake mix (regular size)
2 large eggs
½ cup water

ICING
⅔ cup water
⅓ cup light corn syrup
8 cups confectioners' sugar
1½ teaspoons vanilla extract
2 ounces unsweetened chocolate, chopped
1 to 3 tablespoons warm water

1. In a large bowl, combine the cake mix, eggs and water; beat on low speed for 30 seconds. Beat on medium for 2 minutes.

2. Drop the dough by rounded tablespoonfuls 3 in. apart onto greased baking sheets. Bake at 375° for 8-10 minutes or until the edges begin to brown. Cool for 2 minutes before removing to wire racks to cool completely.

3. For the icing, in a large heavy saucepan, combine the water and corn syrup; bring just to a boil over medium heat. Remove from the heat; whisk in confectioners' sugar and vanilla until smooth.

4. In a small microwave-safe bowl, melt chocolate. Stir in 1 cup of icing and 1 tablespoon warm water until smooth. (Icings will thicken as they stand; stir in more water, 1 teaspoon at a time, to thin if needed.)

5. Spoon chocolate icing over half of each cookie; spread evenly. Spoon the vanilla icing over the remaining half of cookies; spread evenly. Let stand until set.

6. Cut a small hole in the corner of a pastry or plastic bag; insert #2 round pastry tip. Fill the bag with the remaining vanilla icing; pipe a spider web onto the chocolate half of each cookie.

7. Using another bag, pipe spiders onto the cookies with remaining chocolate icing. Let stand until set. Store in an airtight container.

JACK-O'-LANTERN CAKE

PREP: 35 MIN. • **BAKE:** 30 MIN. + COOLING
MAKES: 16 SERVINGS

- **2 packages spice cake mix (regular size)**
- **4 cans (16 ounces each) vanilla frosting**
  Red and yellow food coloring
- **1 ice cream cake cone (about 3 inches tall)**
- **1 package (24 ounces) ready-to-use**
  rolled black fondant
- **2 Oreo cookies**

1. Prepare and bake the cakes according to the package directions using two 10-in. fluted tube pans. Invert cakes onto wire racks; cool completely. Meanwhile, tint frosting orange using red and yellow food coloring.

2. Cut thin slice off bottom of each cake. Spread one cake bottom with frosting; press flat sides together to make a pumpkin shape. Place a foil ball in the center to support the stem; top with an ice cream cake cone. Frost cake with remaining frosting.

3. To decorate face, roll out fondant to ⅛-in. thickness; cut into desired shapes for mouth and nose. Remove tops from two Oreo cookies; cut half-circles in filling for eyes. Press cookies and fondant into frosting to make the face.

I pieced two Bundt cakes together to make this gap-toothed grinner that will make the best-ever centerpiece at your Halloween party.
—JULIANNE JOHNSON GROVE CITY, MN

MINI PRETZEL PUMPKINS

Folks are sure to share some tricks in order to get a taste of these sweet pumpkin-shaped treats.

—TASTE OF HOME TEST KITCHEN

PREP: 30 MIN. + STANDING
MAKES: 2 DOZEN

- ½ **pound white candy coating, coarsely chopped**
- 24 **miniature pretzels**
  Orange colored sugar or sprinkles
- 6 **green gumdrops, cut into four lengthwise slices**

1. In a microwave, melt candy coating; stir until smooth. Dip one pretzel in candy coating; let excess drip off.

2. Place on waxed paper-lined baking sheets. If desired, fill pretzel holes with candy coating. Decorate with orange sugar or sprinkles. For stem, dip the back of one gumdrop piece into candy coating; place above the pumpkin. Repeat. Let pretzels stand until set, about 30 minutes.

BAT CUPCAKES

Even my adult children love these Halloween cupcakes! We serve them every year at our pumpkin-carving party. You can also make them with the fudge stripes on their wings facing up for variety.

—JOYCE MOYNIHAN LAKEVILLE, MN

PREP: 25 MIN. • **BAKE:** 20 MIN. + COOLING
MAKES: 2 DOZEN

- 1 **package chocolate cake mix (regular size)**
- 1 **can (16 ounces) chocolate frosting**
- 24 **fudge-striped cookies**
- 24 **milk chocolate kisses**
   White decorating icing

1. Prepare and bake cake mix according to package directions for cupcakes. Cool completely.

2. Spread the frosting over cupcakes. For the bat wings, cut the cookies in half; insert two cookie halves into each cupcake.

3. Gently press chocolate kisses into frosting for heads. Add eyes with decorating icing.

NOTES

COFFIN ICE CREAM SANDWICHES

START TO FINISH: 20 MIN.
MAKES: 6 SERVINGS

- ½ **cup plus 3 tablespoons vanilla frosting, divided**
  Orange and black paste food coloring
- 6 **ice cream sandwiches**
  Yellow, brown and orange jimmies and/or Halloween sprinkles

Tint ½ cup frosting orange and 1 tablespoon frosting black. Cut corners off each ice cream sandwich to form coffin shapes. Dip sides of sandwiches in jimmies. Frost tops with orange frosting. Decorate as desired with black frosting, remaining white frosting and jimmies and/or sprinkles. Freeze until serving.

These chilling sweets will give your guests the shivers. These coffins are easy to decorate, so your kids can help!
—*TASTE OF HOME* TEST KITCHEN

HALLOWEEN CHOCOLATE COOKIE POPS

Our children look forward to making these cute cookies each year. By now, they have become experts at creating silly faces with little candies.

—KATHY STOCK LEVAY, MO

PREP: 25 MIN. • **BAKE:** 10 MIN./BATCH + COOLING
MAKES: 2 DOZEN

- 1 **cup butter, softened**
- 2 **cups sugar**
- 2 **large eggs**
- 3 **teaspoons vanilla extract**
- 3 **cups all-purpose flour**
- 1 **cup baking cocoa**
- ½ **teaspoon baking powder**
- ½ **teaspoon baking soda**
- ½ **teaspoon salt**
- 24 **lollipop sticks**
  Prepared vanilla frosting
  Food coloring
  Black and yellow decorating gels
  Optional decorations: candy corn, candy eyeballs, M&M's minis and cinnamon hearts

1. Preheat oven to 350°. In a large bowl, beat butter and sugar until blended. Beat in eggs and vanilla. In a small bowl, whisk flour, cocoa, baking powder, baking soda and salt; gradually beat into sugar mixture. Shape dough into 1½-in. balls. Place 3 in. apart on greased baking sheets.
2. Insert a lollipop stick into each cookie. Flatten with a glass dipped in sugar. Bake for 10-12 minutes or until cookies are set. Remove from pans to wire racks to cool completely. Tint frosting; frost cookies. Decorate with gel and optional decorations as desired.

MERINGUE BONES

This unique treatment for meringue travels well, too! You will certainly get requests for the recipe, and folks will be surprised at how simple it is!

—*TASTE OF HOME* TEST KITCHEN

PREP: 30 MIN. • **BAKE:** 1½ HOURS + COOLING
MAKES: 1 DOZEN

- 2 **large egg whites**
- ⅛ **teaspoon cream of tartar**
- ½ **cup sugar**

1. In a small bowl, beat egg whites and cream of tartar on medium speed until soft peaks form. Gradually add sugar, 1 tablespoon at a time, beating on high until stiff peaks form. Place mixture in a heavy-duty resealable plastic bag; cut a small hole in a corner of bag.

2. On parchment-lined baking sheets, pipe meringue into a 3-in. log. Pipe two 1-in. balls on opposite sides of each end of the log. Repeat with remaining meringue. Bake at 225° for 1½ hours or until firm. Remove to wire racks. Store in an airtight container.

NOTES

_____
_____
_____
_____
_____
_____
_____
_____

FUN CARAMEL APPLES

Charming designs and gooey candy make these caramel apples irresistible. Use apples at room temperature because caramel tends to slip off of chilled apples.

—DARLA WESTER MERIDEN, IA

PREP: 30 MIN. + CHILLING
MAKES: 8 SERVINGS

- 1 **package (11½ ounces) milk chocolate chips**
- 2 **tablespoons shortening**
- 1 **package (14 ounces) vibrant green Wilton candy melts**
- 1 **package (14 ounces) white Wilton candy melts**
- 2 **packages (14 ounces each) caramels**
- ¼ **cup water**
- 8 **large tart apples, room temperature**
- 8 **lollipop sticks**
  Assorted candies such as jimmies, M&M's and Reese's Pieces

1. In a microwave-safe bowl, melt chocolate chips and shortening; stir until smooth and set aside. In another microwave-safe bowl, microwave melt the green candy melts. Repeat with white candy melts.

2. In another microwave-safe bowl, microwave the caramels and water, uncovered, on high for 1 minute; stir. Heat 30-45 seconds longer or until caramels are melted; stir until smooth.

3. Line a baking sheet with waxed paper and grease the paper; set aside. Wash and thoroughly dry apples. Insert a stick into each; dip into caramel mixture, turning to coat. Place on prepared pan. Drizzle with melted chocolate and candy melts. Decorate as desired with melted chocolate, candy melts and candies. Refrigerate until set.

REESE'S CHOCOLATE SNACK CAKE

My family constantly requests this cake. Its yellow and orange toppings make it the perfect dessert for a Halloween party. No one will guess it's on the lighter side.

—EILEEN TRAVIS UKIAH, CA

PREP: 15 MIN. • **BAKE:** 30 MIN. + COOLING
MAKES: 20 SERVINGS

- 3⅓ cups all-purpose flour
- ⅔ cup sugar
- ⅔ cup packed brown sugar
- ½ cup baking cocoa
- 2 teaspoons baking soda
- 1 teaspoon salt
- 2 cups water
- ⅓ cup canola oil
- ⅓ cup unsweetened applesauce
- 2 teaspoons white vinegar
- 1 teaspoon vanilla extract
- 1 cup Reese's pieces
- ½ cup coarsely chopped salted peanuts

1. Preheat oven to 350°. Coat a 13x9-in. baking pan with cooking spray.

2. Whisk together first six ingredients. In another bowl, whisk together water, oil, applesauce, vinegar and vanilla. Add to flour mixture, stirring just until blended. Transfer batter to the prepared pan. Sprinkle with Reese's pieces and peanuts.

3. Bake until a toothpick inserted in center comes out clean, 30-35 minutes. Cool on a wire rack.

SWEET & SPICY MUNCH

Kids of all ages love the salty-sweet blend in this fast-to-fix snack mix. Wrap it up in colored paper cones so kids can enjoy it on the go.

—SHANA REILEY THERESA, NY

START TO FINISH: 5 MIN.
MAKES: 2 QUARTS

- 1 **pound spiced gumdrops**
- 1 **pound candy corn**
- 1 **can (16 ounces) salted peanuts**

In a large bowl, combine the gumdrops, candy corn and peanuts. Store in an airtight container.

NOTES

_____
_____
_____
_____
_____
_____
_____

CANDY APPLE PIE

This is the only apple pie my husband will eat, but that's all right since he makes it as often as I do. Like a combination of apple and pecan pie, it's a sweet treat that usually tops off our holiday meals from New Year's all the way through to Christmas!

—CINDY KLEWENO BURLINGTON, CO

PREP: 20 MIN. • **BAKE:** 45 MIN.
MAKES: 8 SERVINGS

- 6 **cups sliced peeled tart apples**
- 2 **tablespoons lime juice**
- ¾ **cup sugar**
- ¼ **cup all-purpose flour**
- ½ **teaspoon ground cinnamon**
- ¼ **teaspoon salt**
  Pastry for double-crust pie (9 inches)
- 2 **tablespoons butter**

TOPPING
- 2 **tablespoons butter**
- ¼ **cup packed brown sugar**
- 1 **tablespoon heavy whipping cream**
- ¼ **cup chopped pecans**

1. In a large bowl, toss apples with lime juice. Combine the sugar, flour, cinnamon and salt; add to the apples and toss lightly.

2. Line a 9-in. pie plate with bottom crust and trim even with edge; fill with apple mixture. Dot with butter. Roll out remaining pastry to fit top of pie. Place over filling. Trim, seal and flute edges; cut slits in pastry.

3. Bake at 400° for 40-45 minutes or until golden brown and apples are tender.

4. For the topping, melt butter in a small saucepan. Stir in the brown sugar and cream; bring it to a boil, stirring constantly. Remove from the heat and stir in pecans.

5. Pour over top crust. Bake 3-4 minutes longer or until bubbly. Place on a wire rack. Serve warm.

POPCORN JACK-O'-LANTERNS

Everyone makes popcorn balls at Christmas, but it's really fun to make them for other occasions, too. The faces on the pumpkins are so cute!

—RUTH PETERSON JENISON, MI

START TO FINISH: 30 MIN.
MAKES: 1 DOZEN

- 3 **quarts popped popcorn**
- ¼ **cup butter, cubed**
- 1 **package (10½ ounces) miniature marshmallows**
- ½ **cup plus 1 to 2 tablespoons marshmallow creme, divided**
- 1 **package (3 ounces) orange gelatin**
- 12 **green Dots candies**
   Green Fruit Roll-Ups
- 18 **each green and brown Tootsie Roll Midgees**

1. Place popcorn in a large bowl. In a large microwave-safe bowl, heat the butter, marshmallows and ½ cup marshmallow creme on high for 1½ to 2 minutes or until melted; stir in gelatin powder until dissolved. Pour over popcorn and toss to coat.

2. With lightly buttered hands, quickly shape mixture into twelve 3-in. balls, flattening one side slightly. For each stem, insert a green Dots candy at the top of a pumpkin, attaching with marshmallow creme. Cut the fruit roll into leaves and vines; attach to top of pumpkin.

3. Warm Tootsie rolls in a microwave for 5-10 seconds, then flatten and cut into facial features as desired; attach with remaining marshmallow creme.

MARTIAN MARSHMALLOWS

PREP: 20 MIN. + STANDING • **COOK:** 10 MIN.
MAKES: 3 DOZEN

- 12 **ounces white candy coating**
- 2 **teaspoons shortening**
  Paste food coloring, optional
- 36 **lollipop sticks**
- 1 **package (10 ounces) large marshmallows (about 36)**
  Colored sugar
  Assorted toppings: candy eyes, assorted nonpareils, licorice and sour straws

1. In a microwave, melt candy coating and shortening; stir until smooth. If desired, tint with food coloring.
2. Insert one lollipop stick into each marshmallow. Dip marshmallows in melted candy coating, turning to coat; allow excess to drip off. Roll in colored sugar. Place a dab of melted candy coating onto assorted toppings; decorate faces as desired. Place on waxed paper; let stand until set.

Wrap leftovers in cellophane and hand them out as favors—if they haven't all disappeared by the end of the party.
—TERI RASEY CADILLAC, MI

SO-EASY-IT'S-SPOOKY BAT CAKE

This gorgeous dessert starts with a boxed cake mix. Then it's an easy and magical trick to make the bat silhouette with cocoa.

—CRYSTAL SCHLUETER BABBITT, MN

PREP: 25 MIN. + CHILLING
BAKE: 25 MIN. + COOLING
MAKES: 16 SERVINGS

1 **devil's food or orange cake mix (regular size)**
1 **teaspoon orange food coloring, optional**

ORANGE FROSTING
4⅔ **cups confectioners' sugar**
1 **cup butter, softened**
2 **teaspoons vanilla extract**
  Orange food coloring
6 **to 7 tablespoons 2% milk**

CHOCOLATE FROSTING
4 **cups confectioners' sugar**
⅔ **cup baking cocoa, sifted**
1 **cup butter, softened**
2 **teaspoons vanilla extract**
6 **to 7 tablespoons 2% milk**
10 **peanut butter cups, finely chopped**
  Dutch-processed cocoa or confectioners' sugar

1. Prepare and bake cake mix according to package directions, using two 9-in. round baking pans. If preparing orange cake, add orange food coloring. Cool as package directs.

2. For bat design, cut a bat pattern from card stock. Wrap with foil.

3. For devil's food cake, prepare the orange frosting by beating the confectioners' sugar, butter, vanilla, food coloring and enough milk to reach a spreading consistency. For orange cake, prepare the chocolate frosting by beating confectioners' sugar, cocoa, butter, vanilla and enough milk for spreading.

4. Using a long serrated knife, trim tops of cakes if domed. Place one cake layer on a serving plate. Spread with 1 cup frosting; sprinkle with chopped candies. Top with the remaining cake layer, bottom side up. Spread remaining frosting over top and sides of cake. Refrigerate until set, about 30 minutes.

5. Lay a bat pattern on top of the cake. Using a fine-mesh strainer, sift Dutch-processed cocoa or confectioners' sugar over frosting. Lift pattern carefully to remove.

FREEZE OPTION *Wrap cooled cake layers in plastic wrap, then cover them securely in foil; freeze. To use, thaw the cakes before unwrapping. Assemble as directed.*

FALL SLOW
COOKER CLASSICS

SPICED CARROTS & BUTTERNUT SQUASH

When I have a lot going on in the kitchen, the slow cooker is my go-to tool for cooking veggies. The sweet squash and carrots really complement the spicy seasonings.

—COURTNEY STULTZ WEIR, KS

PREP: 15 MIN. • **COOK:** 4 HOURS
MAKES: 6 SERVINGS

- 5 **large carrots, cut into ½-inch pieces (about 3 cups)**
- 2 **cups cubed peeled butternut squash (1-inch pieces)**
- 1 **tablespoon balsamic vinegar**
- 1 **tablespoon olive oil**
- 1 **tablespoon honey**
- 1 **teaspoon ground cinnamon**
- ½ **teaspoon salt**
- ½ **teaspoon ground cumin**
- ¼ **teaspoon chili powder**

Place carrots and squash in a 3-qt. slow cooker. In a small bowl, mix remaining ingredients; drizzle over vegetables and toss to coat. Cook, covered, on low for 4-5 hours or until vegetables are tender. Gently stir before serving.

VEGETABLE LENTIL SOUP

Nothing says healthy like this soup, perfect for vegetarians and those watching their weight. Butternut squash and lentils make it filling, while herbs and other veggies round out the flavor.

—MARK MORGAN WATERFORD, WI

PREP: 15 MIN. • **COOK:** 4½ HOURS
MAKES: 6 SERVINGS (ABOUT 2 QUARTS)

- 3 **cups cubed peeled butternut squash**
- 1 **cup chopped carrot**
- 1 **cup chopped onion**
- 1 **cup dried lentils, rinsed**
- 2 **garlic cloves, minced**
- 1 **teaspoon dried oregano**
- 1 **teaspoon dried basil**
- 4 **cups vegetable broth**
- 1 **can (14½ ounces) Italian diced tomatoes, undrained**
- 2 **cups frozen cut green beans (about 8 ounces)**

1. Place first eight ingredients in a 5-qt. slow cooker. Cook, covered, on low until lentils are tender, about 4 hours.
2. Stir in tomatoes and beans. Cook, covered, on high until heated through, about 30 minutes.

BBQ HAM SANDWICHES

Friends love these barbecue sandwiches and often ask me to make them. Since I know they are crowd-pleasers, I double the recipe and serve them at potlucks.
—**DANA KNOX** BUTLER, PA

PREP: 20 MIN. • **COOK:** 2 HOURS
MAKES: 16 SERVINGS

- 3 cups ketchup
- ¾ cup chopped onion
- ¾ cup chopped green pepper
- ¾ cup packed brown sugar
- ½ cup lemon juice
- ⅓ cup Worcestershire sauce
- 1 tablespoon prepared mustard
- 1¼ teaspoons ground allspice
- 1½ teaspoons liquid smoke, optional
- 3 pounds thinly sliced deli ham
- 16 kaiser or ciabatta rolls, split
  Sliced pepperoncini, optional

1. In a large saucepan, combine the first eight ingredients; if desired, stir in liquid smoke. Bring mixture to a boil over medium-high heat. Reduce the heat; simmer, uncovered, for 5 minutes, stirring occasionally.
2. Place ham in a 5- or 6-qt. slow cooker. Add the sauce; stir gently to combine. Cook, covered, on low 2-3 hours or until heated through. Serve on rolls. Top with pepperoncini if desired.

HEARTY SLOW COOKER CHILI

When it's time to build my zesty chili, I combine everything the night before. In the morning, I load the slow cooker and let it do the work.

—MOLLY BUTT GRANVILLE, OH

PREP: 25 MIN. • **COOK:** 6 HOURS
MAKES: 10 SERVINGS (2¾ QUARTS)

- 2 **teaspoons canola oil**
- 1 **large green pepper, chopped**
- 1 **large onion, chopped**
- 2 **garlic cloves, minced**
- 3 **pounds lean ground beef (90% lean)**
- 2 **cans (14½ ounces each) stewed tomatoes, undrained**
- 2 **cans (8 ounces each) tomato sauce**
- 2 **cans (4 ounces each) chopped green chilies**
- ½ **cup minced fresh parsley**
- 2 **tablespoons chili powder**
- 1¼ **teaspoons salt**
- 1 **teaspoon paprika**
- ½ **teaspoon pepper**
  Hot cooked rice or pasta
  Optional toppings: shredded cheddar cheese, sour cream and sliced green onions

1. In a large skillet, heat oil over medium-high heat. Add green pepper, onion and garlic; cook and stir 3-4 minutes or until tender. Transfer to a 6-qt. slow cooker.

2. Working in batches if necessary, cook beef in the same skillet over medium-high heat for 8-10 minutes or until no longer pink, breaking meat into crumbles. Using a slotted spoon, transfer to slow cooker.

3. Stir tomatoes, tomato sauce, chilies, parsley and seasonings into beef mixture. Cook, covered, on low 6-8 hours to allow flavors to blend. Serve chili with rice and toppings as desired.

FREEZE OPTION *Freeze cooled chili in freezer containers. To use, partially thaw in refrigerator overnight. Heat through in a saucepan, stirring occasionally and adding a little water or broth if necessary.*

SLOW COOKER BEEF TIPS BURGUNDY

Here's a heartwarming classic made simple in the slow cooker. Mushrooms, red wine and tender beef make an easy, elegant supper.
—**DEANNA ZEWEN** UNION GROVE, WI

PREP: 15 MIN. • **COOK:** 6¾ HOURS
MAKES: 10 SERVINGS

- 1 **boneless beef chuck roast (3 pounds), trimmed and cut into 1-inch pieces**
- 2 **medium onions, halved and sliced**
- ½ **pound sliced fresh mushrooms**
- 4 **garlic cloves, minced**
- 3 **cups beef stock**
- ½ **cup dry red wine or additional beef stock**
- 2 **tablespoons Worcestershire sauce**
- 2 **tablespoons red wine vinegar**
- 1¼ **teaspoons salt**
- 1 **teaspoon crushed red pepper flakes**
- ½ **teaspoon pepper**
- ⅓ **cup cornstarch**
- ⅓ **cup cold water**
  Hot cooked egg noodles
  Minced fresh parsley

1. In a 5-qt. slow cooker, combine beef, onions, mushrooms and garlic. In a small bowl, mix the next seven ingredients; pour over beef mixture. Cook, covered, on low until meat is tender, 6-8 hours.

2. Skim fat from juices. In a small bowl, mix cornstarch and water until smooth; gradually stir into slow cooker. Cook, covered, on high until thickened, about 45 minutes. Serve with egg noodles; sprinkle with parsley.

FREEZE OPTION *Omitting parsley, freeze the cooled meat mixture, sauce and egg noodles in freezer containers. To use, partially thaw in refrigerator overnight. Microwave, covered, on high in microwave-safe dishes until heated through, stirring gently and adding a little water if necessary. Sprinkle with parsley.*

HELPFUL HINT

A little red wine vinegar adds lift and dimension to the beef sauce. You can substitute balsamic or cider vinegar if you prefer.

CHAI TEA

A wonderful aroma wafts from the slow cooker as this pleasantly sweet and spicy tea cooks.

—CRYSTAL JO BRUNS ILIFF, CO

PREP: 20 MIN. • **COOK:** 8 HOURS
MAKES: 12 SERVINGS (3 QUARTS)

- 15 **slices fresh gingerroot (about 3 ounces)**
- 3 **cinnamon sticks (3 inches)**
- 25 **whole cloves**
- 15 **cardamom pods, lightly crushed**
- 3 **whole peppercorns**
- 3½ **quarts water**
- 8 **black tea bags**
- 1 **can (14 ounces) sweetened condensed milk**

1. Place the first five ingredients on a double thickness of cheesecloth. Gather corners of cloth to enclose seasonings; tie securely with string. Place spice bag and water in a 5- or 6-qt. slow cooker. Cook, covered, on low 8 hours. Discard spice bag.

2. Add tea bags; steep, covered, 3-5 minutes according to taste. Discard the tea bags. Stir in milk and heat through. Serve warm.

HELPFUL HINT

Use spicy or mild Italian sausage in the recipe for a flavor twist. To make the dip a bit lighter, sub in reduced-fat cream cheese and sour cream.

JALAPENO POPPER & SAUSAGE DIP

My workplace had an appetizer contest, and I won it with my jalapeno and cheese dip. Every time I take it to events, folks empty the slow cooker.

—BEV SLABIK DILWORTH, MN

PREP: 15 MIN. • **COOK:** 3 HOURS
MAKES: 24 SERVINGS (¼ CUP EACH)

- 1 **pound bulk spicy pork sausage**
- 2 **packages (8 ounces each) cream cheese, cubed**
- 4 **cups shredded Parmesan cheese (about 12 ounces)**
- 1 **cup (8 ounces) sour cream**
- 1 **can (4 ounces) chopped green chilies, undrained**
- 1 **can (4 ounces) diced jalapeno peppers, undrained**
  Assorted fresh vegetables

1. In a large skillet, cook sausage over medium heat 6-8 minutes or until no longer pink, breaking into crumbles. Using a slotted spoon, transfer sausage to a 3-qt. slow cooker.
2. Stir in cream cheese, Parmesan cheese, sour cream, chilies and peppers. Cook, covered, on low for 3-3½ hours or until heated through. Stir before serving. Serve with vegetables.

SLOW COOKER CHICKEN & DUMPLINGS

Here's a homey dish that people just can't wait to dive into! Yes, you can have chicken and dumplings from the slow cooker. The homemade classic takes a bit of work but is certainly worth it.

—DANIEL ANDERSON KENOSHA, WI

PREP: 20 MIN.
COOK: 6 HOURS + STANDING
MAKES: 8 SERVINGS

- 6 **boneless skinless chicken thighs, chopped**
- ½ **teaspoon salt, divided**
- ½ **teaspoon pepper, divided**
- 1 **tablespoon canola oil**
- 3 **celery ribs, chopped**
- 2 **medium carrots, peeled and chopped**
- 1 **large onion, chopped**
- 3 **garlic cloves, minced**
- 2 **tablespoons tomato paste**
- ⅓ **cup all-purpose flour**
- 4 **cups chicken broth, divided**
- 2 **bay leaves**
- 1 **teaspoon dried thyme**

DUMPLINGS

- 2 **cups all-purpose flour**
- 3 **teaspoons baking powder**
- 1 **teaspoon salt**
- ¼ **teaspoon pepper**
- 1 **cup whole milk**
- 4 **tablespoons melted butter**

1. Sprinkle the chicken with ¼ teaspoon salt and ¼ teaspoon pepper. Meanwhile, in a large skillet, heat oil over medium-high heat. Add chicken; cook and stir until no longer pink, 6-8 minutes. Transfer to a 6-qt. slow cooker.
2. In same skillet, cook celery, carrots and onion until tender, about 6-8 minutes. Add garlic, tomato paste and remaining salt and pepper; cook 1 minute. Stir in flour; cook 1 minute longer. Whisk in 2 cups chicken broth; cook and stir until thickened. Transfer to slow cooker. Stir in bay leaves, thyme and remaining broth.
3. For dumplings, whisk together flour, baking powder, salt and pepper in a large bowl. Stir in milk and butter to form a thick batter. Drop by ¼ cupfuls over chicken mixture. Cook, covered, on low until bubbly and dumplings are set, 6-8 hours. Discard bay leaves. Remove insert and let stand, uncovered, for 15 minutes.

SLOW & EASY MINESTRONE

Hot soup on a cold day is something I just can't get enough of. This minestrone is a snap to put together, and I don't have to wash pots and pans after a relaxing meal.

—SALLY GOEB NEW EGYPT, NJ

PREP: 25 MIN. • **COOK:** 7 HOURS
MAKES: 6 SERVINGS (2¼ QUARTS)

- 1 **can (28 ounces) diced tomatoes, undrained**
- 3 **celery ribs, cut into ½-inch slices**
- 2 **medium carrots, cut into ½-inch slices**
- 2 **small zucchini, halved and cut into ¾-inch slices**
- 2 **cups vegetable broth**
- 1 **cup shredded cabbage**
- ¼ **pound sliced fresh mushrooms**
- 1 **small onion, chopped**
- 2 **garlic cloves, minced**
- 1 **teaspoon dried basil**
- 1 **teaspoon salt**
- ⅓ **cup quick-cooking barley**
- 1 **can (15 ounces) cannellini beans, rinsed and drained**

1. In a 4- or 5-qt. slow cooker, combine the first 11 ingredients. Cover and cook on low for 7-9 hours.
2. Cook barley according to package directions; stir into soup. Add beans; heat through.

CUBAN PULLED PORK SANDWICHES

I lived in Florida for a while and loved the pork I had there, so I went about making it for myself. The flavorful meat makes amazing Cuban sandwiches, but you can also use it in traditional pulled pork sandwiches or tacos.

—LACIE GRIFFIN AUSTIN, TX

PREP: 30 MIN. • **COOK:** 8 HOURS
MAKES: 16 SERVINGS

- 1 cup orange juice
- ½ cup lime juice
- 12 garlic cloves, minced
- 2 tablespoons spiced rum, optional
- 2 tablespoons ground coriander
- 2 teaspoons salt
- 2 teaspoons white pepper
- 2 teaspoons pepper
- 1 teaspoon cayenne pepper
- 5 to 6 pounds boneless pork shoulder roast, cut into four pieces
- 1 tablespoon olive oil

SANDWICHES

- 2 loaves (1 pound each) French bread
  Yellow mustard, optional
- 16 dill pickle slices
- 1½ pounds thinly sliced deli ham
- 1½ pounds Swiss cheese, sliced

1. In a 6- or 7-qt. slow cooker, combine the first nine ingredients. Add pork; cook, covered, on low until tender, 8-10 hours. Remove roast; shred with two forks. In a large skillet, heat oil over medium-high heat. Cook meat in batches until lightly browned and crisp in spots.

2. Cut each loaf of bread in half lengthwise. If desired, spread mustard over cut sides of bread. Layer bottom halves of bread with pickles, pork, ham and cheese. Replace tops. Cut each loaf into eight slices.

SLOW COOKER SAUSAGE & WAFFLE BAKE

Nothing is missing from this sweet and savory combination, guaranteed to create excitement at the breakfast table. It's so wrong, it's right!

—COURTNEY LENTZ BOSTON, MA

PREP: 20 MIN. • **COOK:** 5 HOURS + STANDING
MAKES: 12 SERVINGS

- 2 **pounds bulk spicy breakfast pork sausage**
- 1 **tablespoon rubbed sage**
- ½ **teaspoon fennel seed**
- 1 **package (12.3 ounces) frozen waffles, cut into bite-size pieces**
- 8 **large eggs**
- 1¼ cups **half-and-half cream**
- ¼ **cup maple syrup**
- ¼ **teaspoon salt**
- ¼ **teaspoon pepper**
- 2 **cups shredded cheddar cheese**
  Additional maple syrup

1. Fold two 18-in.-long pieces of foil into two 18x4-in. strips. Line the sides around the perimeter of a 5-qt. slow cooker with foil strips; spray with cooking spray.

2. In a large skillet, cook and crumble sausage over medium heat; drain. Add sage and fennel.

3. Place waffles in slow cooker; top with sausage. In a bowl, mix eggs, cream, syrup and seasonings. Pour over sausage and waffles. Top with shredded cheese. Cook, covered, on low until set, 5-6 hours. Remove insert and let stand, uncovered, 15 minutes. Serve with additional maple syrup.

SLOW COOKER BACON MAC & CHEESE

PREP: 20 MIN. • **COOK:** 3 HOURS + STANDING
MAKES: 18 SERVINGS (½ CUP EACH)

- 2 **large eggs, lightly beaten**
- 4 **cups whole milk**
- 1 **can (12 ounces) evaporated milk**
- ¼ **cup butter, melted**
- 1 **tablespoon all-purpose flour**
- 1 **teaspoon salt**
- 1 **package (16 ounces) small pasta shells**
- 1 **cup shredded provolone cheese**
- 1 **cup shredded Manchego or Monterey Jack cheese**
- 1 **cup shredded white cheddar cheese**
- 8 **bacon strips, cooked and crumbled**

1. In a large bowl, whisk the first six ingredients until blended. Stir in pasta and cheeses; transfer to a 4- or 5-qt. slow cooker.

2. Cook, covered, on low 3-3½ hours or until pasta is tender. Turn off slow cooker; remove insert. Let stand, uncovered, 15 minutes before serving. Top with bacon.

I'm all about easy meals from the slow cooker. Using more cheese than ever, I developed an addictive spin on this casserole favorite.
—**KRISTEN HEIGL** STATEN ISLAND, NY

MOIST & TENDER TURKEY BREAST

The first time I slow-cooked turkey was on a vacation. It simmered while we were out, and we came back to a spectacularly juicy bird.
—**HEIDI VAWDREY** RIVERTON, UT

PREP: 10 MIN. • **COOK:** 4 HOURS
MAKES: 12 SERVINGS

- 1 **bone-in turkey breast (6 to 7 pounds)**
- 4 **fresh rosemary sprigs**
- 4 **garlic cloves, peeled**
- ½ **cup water**
- 1 **tablespoon brown sugar**
- ½ **teaspoon coarsely ground pepper**
- ¼ **teaspoon salt**

Place turkey breast, rosemary, garlic and water in a 6-qt. slow cooker. Mix brown sugar, pepper and salt; sprinkle over turkey. Cook, covered, on low 4-6 hours or until turkey is tender and a thermometer inserted in turkey reads at least 170°.

ALL-DAY APPLE BUTTER

PREP: 20 MIN. • **COOK:** 11 HOURS
MAKES: 4 PINTS

5½ pounds apples, peeled and finely chopped
4 cups sugar
2 to 3 teaspoons ground cinnamon
¼ teaspoon ground cloves
¼ teaspoon salt

1. Place apples in a 3-qt. slow cooker. Combine sugar, cinnamon, cloves and salt; pour over apples and mix well. Cover and cook on high for 1 hour.
2. Reduce heat to low; cover and cook for 9-11 hours or until thickened and dark brown, stirring occasionally (stir more frequently as it thickens to prevent sticking).
3. Uncover and cook on low 1 hour longer. If desired, stir with a wire whisk until smooth. Spoon into freezer containers, leaving ½-in. headspace. Cover and refrigerate or freeze.

I make several batches of this simple and delicious apple butter to freeze in jars. Depending on the sweetness of the apples used, you can adjust the sugar to taste.

—BETTY RUENHOLL SYRACUSE, NE

APPLE PIE OATMEAL DESSERT

This warm and comforting dessert brings back memories of time spent with my family around the kitchen table. I serve the dish with sweetened whipped cream or vanilla ice cream as a topper.

—CAROL GREER EARLVILLE, IL

PREP: 15 MIN. • **COOK:** 4 HOURS
MAKES: 6 SERVINGS

- 1 **cup quick-cooking oats**
- ½ **cup all-purpose flour**
- ⅓ **cup packed brown sugar**
- 2 **teaspoons baking powder**
- 1½ **teaspoons apple pie spice**
- ¼ **teaspoon salt**
- 3 **large eggs**
- 1⅔ **cups 2% milk, divided**
- 1½ **teaspoons vanilla extract**
- 3 **medium apples, peeled and finely chopped**
  Vanilla ice cream, optional

1. In a large bowl, whisk oats, flour, brown sugar, baking powder, pie spice and salt. In a small bowl, whisk eggs, 1 cup milk and vanilla until blended. Add to oat mixture, stirring just until moistened. Fold in apples.

2. Transfer to a greased 3-qt. slow cooker. Cook, covered, on low 4-5 hours or until apples are tender and top is set.

3. Stir in remaining milk. Serve warm or cold, with ice cream if desired.

AUTUMN APPLE CHICKEN

Back from apple picking, I wanted to bake something new with the bounty. Slow-cooking chicken with apples and barbecue sauce filled my whole house with the most delicious smell. We couldn't wait to eat.

—CAITLYN HAUSER BROOKLINE, NH

PREP: 20 MIN. • **COOK:** 3½ HOURS
MAKES: 4 SERVINGS

- 1 **tablespoon canola oil**
- 4 **bone-in chicken thighs (about 1½ pounds), skin removed**
- ¼ **teaspoon salt**
- ¼ **teaspoon pepper**
- 2 **medium Fuji or Gala apples, coarsely chopped**
- 1 **medium onion, chopped**
- 1 **garlic clove, minced**
- ⅓ **cup barbecue sauce**
- ¼ **cup apple cider or juice**
- 1 **tablespoon honey**

1. In a large skillet, heat oil over medium heat. Brown chicken thighs on both sides; sprinkle with salt and pepper. Transfer to a 3-qt. slow cooker; top with apples.
2. Add onion to same skillet; cook and stir over medium heat 2-3 minutes or until tender. Add garlic; cook 1 minute longer. Stir in barbecue sauce, apple cider and honey; increase heat to medium-high. Cook 1 minute, stirring to loosen browned bits from pan. Pour over chicken and apples. Cook, covered, on low 3½-4½ hours or until chicken is tender.
FREEZE OPTION *Freeze cooled chicken mixture in freezer containers. To use, partially thaw in refrigerator overnight. Heat through in a covered saucepan, stirring occasionally.*

FIVE-STAR
PUMPKIN
FAVORITES

GREAT PUMPKIN DESSERT

Here's a crowd-pleasing alternative to pumpkin pie that always gets compliments and requests for the recipe. And it's so easy!

—LINDA GUYOT FOUNTAIN VALLEY, CA

PREP: 5 MIN. • **BAKE:** 1 HOUR
MAKES: 16 SERVINGS

- 1 **can (15 ounces) solid-pack pumpkin**
- 1 **can (12 ounces) evaporated milk**
- 3 **large eggs**
- 1 **cup sugar**
- 4 **teaspoons pumpkin pie spice**
- 1 **package yellow cake mix (regular size)**
- ¾ **cup butter, melted**
- 1½ **cups chopped walnuts**
  Vanilla ice cream or whipped cream

1. In a large bowl, beat the first five ingredients until smooth.

2. Transfer to a greased 13x9-in. baking dish. Sprinkle with cake mix and drizzle with butter. Top with walnuts.

3. Bake at 350° for 1 hour or until a knife inserted in the center comes out clean. Serve dessert with ice cream or whipped cream.

PECAN PUMPKIN CHEESECAKE

I love to play with cheesecakes by mixing and matching flavors. This one with pumpkin and maple is the star of our Thanksgiving spread.

—SUE GRONHOLZ BEAVER DAM, WI

PREP: 30 MIN.
BAKE: 70 MIN. + CHILLING
MAKES: 16 SERVINGS

- 1 **cup graham cracker crumbs**
- 3 **tablespoons granulated sugar**
- 2 **tablespoons butter, melted**

FILLING

- 3 **packages (8 ounces each) cream cheese, softened**
- ½ **cup packed brown sugar**
- ⅓ **cup granulated sugar**
- ¼ **cup maple syrup**
- 3 **large eggs, room temperature**
- 1 **can (15 ounces) solid-pack pumpkin**
- 2 **tablespoons cornstarch**
- 3 **teaspoons vanilla extract**
- 1½ **teaspoons pumpkin pie spice**

TOPPING

- 1 **cup heavy whipping cream**
- ¾ **cup maple syrup**
- ½ **cup chopped pecans, toasted**

1. Preheat oven to 325°. Wrap a double thickness of heavy-duty foil (about 18 in. square) around a greased 9-in. springform pan. Mix cracker crumbs and granulated sugar; stir in butter. Press onto bottom of prepared pan.

2. Beat cream cheese, sugars and maple syrup until smooth. Add eggs; beat on low just until blended. Whisk in pumpkin, cornstarch, vanilla and pumpkin pie spice; pour over crust. Place springform pan in a larger baking pan; add 1 in. of hot water to larger pan.

3. Bake until center is just set and top appears dull, 70-80 minutes. Remove springform pan from water bath. Cool cheesecake on a wire rack 10 minutes. Loosen sides from pan with a knife; remove foil. Cool cheesecake for 1 hour longer. Refrigerate overnight, covering when completely cooled.

4. For topping, combine whipping cream and maple syrup in a small saucepan over medium heat; bring to a boil. Continue boiling, stirring occasionally, until slightly thickened, 15-20 minutes. Stir in the toasted pecans. Refrigerate until cold.

5. Remove rim from pan. Stir topping; spoon over cheesecake.

NOTE *To toast nuts, bake in a shallow pan in a 350° oven for 5-10 minutes or cook in a skillet over low heat until lightly browned, stirring occasionally.*

BREAD MACHINE PUMPKIN MONKEY BREAD

I love making this pumpkin bread straight from my bread machine. Leftovers reheat well on busy weekdays, and any extra sauce makes an excellent pancake or waffle syrup.

—EMILY MAIN TONOPAH, AZ

PREP: 45 MIN. + RISING
BAKE: 20 MIN. + COOLING
MAKES: 18 SERVINGS

- 1 **cup warm 2% milk (70° to 80°)**
- ¾ **cup canned pumpkin**
- 2 **tablespoons butter, softened**
- ¼ **cup sugar**
- 1 **teaspoon salt**
- 1 **teaspoon ground cinnamon**
- ½ **teaspoon ground ginger**
- ¼ **teaspoon ground cloves**
- ¼ **teaspoon ground nutmeg**
- 4 **to 4¼ cups all-purpose flour**
- 2 **teaspoons active dry yeast**

SAUCE
- 1 **cup butter, cubed**
- 1 **cup packed brown sugar**
- 1 **cup dried cranberries**
- ¼ **cup canned pumpkin**
- 1 **teaspoon ground cinnamon**
- ½ **teaspoon ground ginger**
- ¼ **teaspoon ground nutmeg**
- ¼ **teaspoon ground cloves**

1. In bread machine pan, place the first 11 ingredients in order suggested by manufacturer. Select dough setting. Check dough after 5 minutes of mixing; add 1-2 tablespoons of water or flour if needed.

2. Meanwhile, in a large saucepan, combine sauce ingredients; cook and stir until blended. Remove from the heat.

3. When dough cycle is completed, turn dough onto a lightly floured surface. Divide into 36 portions; shape into balls.

4. Arrange half of the balls in a greased 10-in. fluted tube pan; cover with half of the sauce. Repeat, being sure to thoroughly coat the top layer with sauce.

5. Let rise in a warm place until doubled, about 30 minutes. Preheat oven to 375°. Bake 20-25 minutes or until golden brown. Cover loosely with foil if top browns too quickly.

6. Cool in pan 10 minutes before inverting onto a serving plate. Serve bread warm.

NOTE *We recommend you do not use a bread machine's time-delay feature for this recipe.*

PUMPKIN PATCH BISCUITS

I often make a double batch of these fluffy biscuits to meet the demand. My father loves them so much he requests them for Christmas, Father's Day and his birthday!

—LIZA TAYLOR SEATTLE, WA

PREP: 20 MIN. • **BAKE:** 20 MIN.
MAKES: 6 BISCUITS

- 1¾ cups all-purpose flour
- ¼ cup packed brown sugar
- 2½ teaspoons baking powder
- ½ teaspoon salt
- ¼ teaspoon baking soda
- ½ cup plus 1½ teaspoons cold butter, divided
- ¾ cup canned pumpkin
- ⅓ cup buttermilk

1. In a large bowl, combine flour, brown sugar, baking powder, salt and baking soda. Cut in ½ cup butter until mixture resembles coarse crumbs. Combine pumpkin and buttermilk; stir into the crumb mixture just until moistened.

2. Turn onto a lightly floured surface; knead 8-10 times. Pat or roll out to 1-in. thickness; cut with a floured 2½-in. biscuit cutter. Place 1 in. apart on a greased baking sheet.

3. Bake at 425° for 18-22 minutes or until golden brown. Melt remaining butter; brush over biscuits. Serve warm.

SOUR CREAM-PUMPKIN COFFEE CAKE

Spiced pumpkin filling is the sweet surprise inside this coffee cake. It's sure to steal the spotlight at a fall breakfast or brunch.

—RACHEL DODD AVONDALE, AZ

PREP: 30 MIN.
BAKE: 45 MIN. + COOLING
MAKES: 15 SERVINGS

- 1 **cup packed brown sugar**
- ¼ **cup all-purpose flour**
- 2 **teaspoons pumpkin pie spice**
- ⅓ **cup cold butter**
- 1 **cup chopped pecans**

BATTER

- ½ **cup butter, softened**
- ¾ **cup sugar**
- 3 **large eggs**
- 1 **teaspoon vanilla extract**
- 2 **cups all-purpose flour**
- 1 **teaspoon baking powder**
- 1 **teaspoon baking soda**
- 1 **cup (8 ounces) sour cream**

FILLING

- 1 **can (15 ounces) solid-pack pumpkin**
- 1 **large egg, lightly beaten**
- ⅓ **cup sugar**
- 1 **teaspoon pumpkin pie spice**

1. Preheat oven to 325°. For streusel, in a small bowl, combine brown sugar, flour and pumpkin pie spice. Cut in butter until crumbly. Stir in pecans; set aside.

2. In a large bowl, cream butter and sugar until light and fluffy. Beat in the eggs, one at a time, and vanilla. Combine flour, baking powder and baking soda; add to creamed mixture alternately with sour cream.

3. Spread half of the batter into a greased 13x9-in. baking dish. Sprinkle with half of the streusel. Combine pumpkin, egg, sugar and pumpkin pie spice; drop by tablespoonfuls over streusel and spread evenly. Top with remaining batter and streusel.

4. Bake 45-50 minutes or until a toothpick inserted in center comes out clean. Cool on a wire rack.

CHEESE & PUMPKIN-FILLED MANICOTTI

Our family adores autumn and anything to do with pumpkins! This warm, comforting recipe is so easy to put together on a cool fall weeknight. When I have time, I make homemade ravioli and tortellini using this same filling. It also works well in stuffed shells.

—MANDY HOWISON RENFREW, PA

PREP: 30 MIN. • **BAKE:** 25 MIN.
MAKES: 7 SERVINGS

- 1 **package (8 ounces) manicotti shells**
- 1 **container (15 ounces) ricotta cheese**
- 2 **cups shredded part-skim mozzarella cheese, divided**
- 1 **cup canned pumpkin**
- ¼ **cup grated Parmesan cheese**
- 2 **large egg yolks**
- ¼ **teaspoon ground nutmeg**
- 1 **jar (24 ounces) garlic spaghetti sauce, divided**

1. Preheat oven to 350°. Cook the manicotti shells according to the package directions for al dente. Drain.

2. In a large bowl, mix ricotta cheese, 1 cup mozzarella cheese, pumpkin, Parmesan cheese, egg yolks and nutmeg. Spoon into manicotti.

3. Spread 1 cup spaghetti sauce into a greased 13x9-in. baking dish. Top with stuffed manicotti. Pour remaining spaghetti sauce over top; sprinkle with remaining mozzarella cheese. Bake, covered, 25-30 minutes or until cheese is melted.

RUSTIC PUMPKIN BREAD

I received this pumpkin bread recipe from a co-worker who made it for an office party. It is so yummy and moist that I now make it every year at the holidays for friends and family.

—SANDY SANDAVAL SANDY VALLEY, NV

PREP: 25 MIN.
BAKE: 1 HOUR + COOLING
MAKES: 2 LOAVES (16 SLICES EACH)

- 3 **cups sugar**
- 1 **can (15 ounces) solid-pack pumpkin**
- 1 **cup canola oil**
- 4 **large eggs**
- ⅔ **cup water**
- 3½ **cups all-purpose flour**
- 2 **teaspoons baking soda**
- 1 **teaspoon salt**
- 1 **teaspoon ground cinnamon**
- 1 **teaspoon ground nutmeg**
- ½ **teaspoon ground cloves**
- ½ **cup chopped pecans**

TOPPING
- ⅓ **cup all-purpose flour**
- ¼ **cup packed brown sugar**
- ½ **teaspoon ground cinnamon**
- 2 **tablespoons cold butter**
- ¼ **cup chopped pecans**

1. In a large bowl, beat the sugar, pumpkin, oil, eggs and water until blended. In a large bowl, combine the flour, baking soda, salt, cinnamon, nutmeg and cloves; gradually beat into pumpkin mixture until blended. Stir in the pecans.

2. Pour into two greased 9x5-in. loaf pans. For topping, in a small bowl, combine the flour, brown sugar and cinnamon; cut in butter until mixture resembles coarse crumbs. Stir in pecans. Sprinkle over batter.

3. Bake at 350° for 60-65 minutes or until a toothpick inserted in center comes out clean. Cool for 10 minutes before removing from pans to wire racks.

CRANBERRY PUMPKIN BREAD
Fold in 1½ cups fresh or thawed frozen cranberries with the pecans.

PISTACHIO PUMPKIN BREAD
Substitute pistachios for pecans in the batter and topping.

PUMPKIN CHIP BREAD
Fold in 1 cup miniature semisweet chocolate chips with the pecans.

BUTTERMILK PUMPKIN WAFFLES

My girlfriend loves pumpkin, so I often like to incorporate the ingredient in my recipes. In fall, I freeze pumpkin puree just to make these waffles.

—CHARLES INSLER SILVER SPRING, MD

PREP: 20 MIN. • **COOK:** 5 MIN./BATCH
MAKES: 6 SERVINGS

- ¾ cup all-purpose flour
- ½ cup whole wheat flour
- 2 tablespoons brown sugar
- 1 teaspoon baking powder
- 1 teaspoon ground cinnamon
- ½ teaspoon ground ginger
- ¼ teaspoon baking soda
- ¼ teaspoon salt
- ¼ teaspoon ground cloves
- 2 large eggs
- 1¼ cups buttermilk
- ½ cup fresh or canned pumpkin
- 2 tablespoons butter, melted
  Butter and maple syrup, optional

1. In a large bowl, combine the first nine ingredients. In a small bowl, whisk the eggs, buttermilk, pumpkin and melted butter. Stir into the dry ingredients just until moistened.

2. Bake in a preheated waffle iron according to the manufacturer's directions until golden brown. Serve with butter and syrup if desired.

FREEZE OPTION *Cool waffles on wire racks. Freeze between layers of waxed paper in a resealable plastic freezer bag. To use, reheat waffles in a toaster on medium setting. Or, microwave each waffle on high for 30-60 seconds or until heated through.*

CRUMB-TOPPED APPLE & PUMPKIN PIE

This special recipe combines all the warm, delicious flavors of the fall season, and it makes a truly unique presentation. It has become a holiday tradition at our house.

—**TRISHA FOX** PLAINFIELD, IL

PREP: 35 MIN.
BAKE: 50 MIN. + COOLING
MAKES: 10 SERVINGS

- 1 **sheet refrigerated pie crust**
- 2 **cups thinly sliced peeled tart apples**
- ¼ **cup sugar**
- 2 **teaspoons all-purpose flour**
- 1 **teaspoon lemon juice**
- ¼ **teaspoon ground cinnamon**

PUMPKIN FILLING

- 1½ **cups canned pumpkin**
- 1 **cup fat-free evaporated milk**
- ½ **cup egg substitute**
- ½ **cup sugar**
- ¾ **teaspoon ground cinnamon**
- ¼ **teaspoon salt**
- ⅛ **teaspoon ground nutmeg**

TOPPING

- ½ **cup all-purpose flour**
- 3 **tablespoons sugar**
- 4½ **teaspoons cold butter**
- 3 **tablespoons chopped walnuts**

1. On a lightly floured surface, unroll crust. Transfer crust to a 9-in. deep-dish pie plate. Trim crust to ½ in. beyond edge of plate; flute edges. In a large bowl, combine the apples, sugar, flour, lemon juice and cinnamon. Spoon into crust.

2. In another large bowl, whisk the pumpkin filling ingredients. Pour over apple mixture. Bake at 375° for 30 minutes.

3. For topping, combine flour and sugar. Cut in butter until crumbly; stir in walnuts. Sprinkle over pie.

4. Bake 20-25 minutes longer or until a knife inserted into pumpkin layer comes out clean (cover edge with foil during the last 15 minutes of baking to prevent overbrowning if necessary).

5. Cool on a wire rack. Refrigerate the leftovers.

TUSCAN TURKEY SOUP

START TO FINISH: 30 MIN.
MAKES: 8 SERVINGS (2 QUARTS)

2 **tablespoons olive oil**
1 **cup chopped onion**
1 **cup chopped celery**
2 **garlic cloves, minced**
2 **cans (14½ ounces each) reduced-sodium chicken broth**
1 **can (15 ounces) solid-pack pumpkin**
1 **can (15 ounces) white kidney or cannellini beans, rinsed and drained**
2 **cups cubed cooked turkey**
½ **teaspoon salt**
½ **teaspoon dried basil**
¼ **teaspoon pepper**
   Grated Parmesan cheese, optional

1. In a large saucepan, heat oil over medium-high heat. Add onion and celery; cook and stir until tender. Add garlic; cook 1 minute longer.

2. Stir in broth, pumpkin, beans, turkey, salt, basil and pepper. Heat through, stirring occasionally. If desired, serve with cheese.

Transform leftover turkey into a uniquely flavored pumpkin soup that's sure to satisfy hungry family and friends. It's so easy, even a beginner cook can make it.

—MARIE MCCONNELL SHELBYVILLE, IL

SPICED PUMPKIN CUSTARD PIE

If you get nervous about making pie crusts, this recipe is for you. All you have to do is pat the nutty, gingery crumb crust into the pie plate.

—CHARLENE CHAMBERS

ORMOND BEACH, FL

PREP: 25 MIN.
BAKE: 40 MIN. + COOLING
MAKES: 8 SERVINGS

- ¾ cup chopped pecans, toasted
- 1 cup plus 2 tablespoons all-purpose flour
- ½ teaspoon ground ginger
- ½ teaspoon salt
- 7 tablespoons shortening
- 2 tablespoons plus 1 teaspoon ice water

FILLING

- 2 large eggs
- ¾ cup sugar
- 1 teaspoon ground cinnamon
- ¾ teaspoon ground allspice
- ½ teaspoon ground ginger
- ½ teaspoon salt
- 1 can (15 ounces) solid-pack pumpkin
- 1 can (12 ounces) evaporated milk
  Whipped cream, optional
  Additional ground cinnamon, optional

1. Place pecans in a food processor; cover and process until finely ground. In a large bowl, combine the pecans, flour, ginger and salt. Cut in shortening until mixture is crumbly. Gradually add water, tossing with a fork until dough forms a ball. Press dough onto the bottom and up the sides of an ungreased 9-in. pie plate.

2. For filling, in a large bowl, beat the eggs, sugar, spices and salt until smooth. Beat in pumpkin. Gradually beat in milk. Pour into the crust.

3. Bake at 400° for 40-45 minutes or until a knife inserted in the center comes out clean. Cover edges with foil during the last 15 minutes of baking to prevent overbrowning if necessary. Cool on a wire rack. Garnish with whipped cream and additional cinnamon if desired. Refrigerate leftovers.

PUMPKIN TIRAMISU

I added pumpkin flavor and subtracted some of the coffee flavor in a tiramisu I developed for a special holiday dinner. A new Christmas tradition was born!

—**HEATHER CLARY** DOWNINGTOWN, PA

PREP: 30 MIN. + CHILLING • **COOK:** 5 MIN.
MAKES: 12 SERVINGS

- 1 **cup water**
- 1 **cup brewed coffee**
- ⅔ **cup sugar**
- ⅔ **cup hazelnut liqueur**

PUMPKIN MIXTURE
- 2 **cartons (8 ounces each) mascarpone cheese**
- ¾ **cup canned pumpkin**
- 5 **tablespoons sugar, divided**
- 1½ **teaspoons ground cinnamon**
- ½ **teaspoon ground nutmeg**
- ¼ **teaspoon ground ginger**
- ¼ **teaspoon ground allspice**
- 1¼ **cups heavy whipping cream**

ASSEMBLY
- 54 **crisp ladyfinger cookies (about 16 ounces)**
- 1 **tablespoon sugar**
- ½ **teaspoon ground cinnamon**

1. In a small saucepan, combine water, coffee, sugar and liqueur; cook and stir over medium-low heat until the sugar is dissolved, about 3 minutes. Transfer to a shallow bowl; cool completely.

2. In a large bowl, mix mascarpone cheese, pumpkin, 3 tablespoons sugar and spices just until blended. In a small bowl, beat cream until it begins to thicken. Add remaining sugar; beat until soft peaks form. Fold into mascarpone mixture.

3. Quickly dip 18 ladyfingers into coffee mixture, allowing excess to drip off. Arrange in a single layer in a 13x9-in. dish. Spread with 1⅔ cups cheese mixture. Repeat layers twice.

4. Mix sugar and cinnamon; sprinkle over top. Refrigerate tiramisu, covered, at least 8 hours or overnight.

NOTE *This recipe was made with Alessi brand ladyfinger cookies.*

SPICED PUMPKIN DOUGHNUT BITES

You can try different flavors and coating colors in this recipe to suit any occasion. For Halloween at my house, it just has to be pumpkin flavor and orange candy coating!

—JOHNNA JOHNSON SCOTTSDALE, AZ

PREP: 35 MIN.
BAKE: 10 MIN./BATCH + COOLING
MAKES: 2 DOZEN

- 1⅓ cups all-purpose flour
- 1 cup Rice Krispies
- 3 tablespoons plus ½ cup sugar, divided
- 3 teaspoons baking powder
- 2½ teaspoons pumpkin pie spice, divided
- ½ teaspoon salt
- ¼ cup butter-flavored shortening
- ⅓ cup canned pumpkin
- ¼ cup 2% milk
- ¼ cup butter
- ¾ cup orange candy coating disks
  Chocolate or Halloween sprinkles, optional

1. Preheat oven to 375°. In a large bowl, mix flour, Rice Krispies, 3 tablespoons sugar, baking powder, 1 teaspoon pie spice and salt; cut in shortening until mixture resembles coarse crumbs. In another bowl, whisk the canned pumpkin and milk; stir into crumb mixture just until moistened.

2. In a microwave, melt butter. In a shallow bowl, mix the remaining sugar and pie spice. Shape level tablespoons of dough into balls. Dip in butter, then roll in sugar mixture. Place 1 in. apart on parchment paper-lined baking sheets.

3. Bake 10-13 minutes or until tops are cracked. Remove from pans to wire racks to cool completely.

4. In a microwave, melt candy coating; stir until smooth. Dip one end of each doughnut bite into melted candy coating, allowing excess to drip off. If desired, decorate with sprinkles. Place on waxed paper; let stand until set.

MINI PUMPKIN CAKES

I saw these cute cakes at a grocery store and decided to make my own version at home. They're a hit at any fall gathering.

—JENNIFER DORFF WAUKESHA, WI

PREP: 1½ HOURS
BAKE: 20 MIN. + STANDING
MAKES: 1 DOZEN

- 1 **package spice cake mix (regular size)**
- 1 **package (3.4 ounces) instant vanilla pudding mix**
- 1 **teaspoon ground cinnamon**
- 4 **large eggs**
- 1 **cup canned pumpkin**
- ½ **cup milk**
- ½ **cup canola oil**
- ¾ **cup chopped walnuts**

ORANGE GLAZE

- 7½ **cups confectioners' sugar**
- ⅔ **cup plus 2 tablespoons water**
- 1 **teaspoon maple flavoring**
  Red and yellow food coloring

GARNISH

- 3 **cups confectioners' sugar**
- 3 **tablespoons water**
  Green food coloring
- 4 **Tootsie Rolls (2¼ ounces and 6 inches each), cut into 2-inch pieces**

1. In a large bowl, combine the first seven ingredients. Beat on low speed for 30 seconds; beat on medium for 2 minutes. Fold in walnuts. Spoon by ½ cupfuls into 12 greased miniature fluted tube pans. Bake at 350° until set, about 20-25 minutes. Cool for 10 minutes before removing from pans to wire racks to cool completely.

2. For the glaze, in a large bowl, beat the confectioners' sugar, water and maple flavoring until smooth; tint orange with red and yellow food coloring. Place wire racks with cakes over waxed paper. Spoon half of the glaze evenly over tops and sides of cakes, letting excess drip off. Let stand until glaze is set. Repeat with remaining glaze.

3. For the garnish, in a small bowl, beat the confectioners' sugar and water until smooth; tint green. Cut a small hole in the corner of a pastry or plastic bag; insert a #4 round pastry tip. Fill bag with green frosting. Pipe vines on the pumpkins. For stem, insert a Tootsie Roll piece in the center of each pumpkin.

MOCHA PUMPKIN SEEDS

Roasted pumpkin seeds are a classic fall snack. Kick them up a notch with instant coffee and cocoa powder for a mix that's mocha genius.

—REBEKAH BEYER SABETHA, KS

PREP: 5 MIN.
BAKE: 20 MIN. + COOLING
MAKES: 3 CUPS

- 6 **tablespoons sugar**
- 2 **tablespoons baking cocoa**
- 1 **tablespoon instant coffee granules**
- 1 **large egg white**
- 2 **cups salted shelled pumpkin seeds (pepitas)**

1. Preheat oven to 325°. Place sugar, cocoa and coffee granules in a small food processor; cover and pulse until finely ground.

2. In a bowl, whisk egg white until frothy. Stir in pumpkin seeds. Sprinkle with sugar mixture; toss to coat evenly. Spread in a single layer in a parchment paper-lined 15x10x1-in. baking pan.

3. Bake 20-25 minutes or until dry and no longer sticky, stirring every 10 minutes. Cool completely in pan. Store in an airtight container.

NEW ENGLAND WALNUT BREAD

Pumpkin bread is for chilly mornings when you long for some home-style New England food. Serve slices with a warm and soothing beverage.

—KIMBERLY FORNI LACONIA, NH

PREP: 25 MIN.
BAKE: 1 HOUR + COOLING
MAKES: 2 LOAVES (16 SLICES EACH)

- ½ cup old-fashioned oats
- ¼ teaspoon sugar
- ⅛ teaspoon ground cinnamon

BREAD

- 1 can (15 ounces) solid-pack pumpkin
- 4 large eggs
- ¾ cup canola oil
- ⅔ cup water
- 2 cups sugar
- 1 cup honey
- 1½ teaspoons vanilla extract
- 3½ cups all-purpose flour
- 2 teaspoons baking soda
- 1½ teaspoons salt
- 1½ teaspoons ground cinnamon
- 1 teaspoon ground nutmeg
- ½ teaspoon ground cloves
- ½ teaspoon ground ginger
- 1 cup coarsely chopped walnuts, toasted

1. Preheat oven to 350°. In a small skillet, combine oats, sugar and cinnamon; cook and stir over medium heat 4-6 minutes or until oats are toasted. Remove from heat.

2. For bread, in a large bowl, beat pumpkin, eggs, oil, water, sugar, honey and vanilla until well blended. In another bowl, whisk flour, baking soda, salt and spices; gradually beat into pumpkin mixture. Fold in walnuts.

3. Transfer to two greased 9x5-in. loaf pans. Sprinkle tops with the oat mixture.

4. Bake 60-70 minutes or until a toothpick inserted in center comes out clean. Cool bread in the pan for 10 minutes before removing to a wire rack to cool.

NOTE *To toast nuts, bake in a shallow pan in a 350° oven for 5-10 minutes or cook in a skillet over low heat until lightly browned, stirring occasionally.*

PUMPKIN PANCAKES WITH SWEET APPLE CIDER SYRUP

The flavors of autumn star in these delightful pumpkin pancakes topped with a sweet apple cider syrup. Light and fluffy, the pancakes are perfect for breakfast or brunch or as a tasty snack anytime!

—**BRENDA PARKER** PORTAGE, MI

PREP: 35 MIN. + STANDING
COOK: 10 MIN.
MAKES: 15 PANCAKES (1 CUP SYRUP)

HOT CIDER SYRUP
- ¾ cup apple cider or juice
- ½ cup packed brown sugar
- ½ cup corn syrup
- 2 tablespoons butter
- ½ teaspoon lemon juice
- ⅛ teaspoon ground cinnamon
- ⅛ teaspoon ground nutmeg

PANCAKES
- 1 cup all-purpose flour
- 1 tablespoon sugar
- 2 teaspoons baking powder
- ½ teaspoon salt
- ½ teaspoon ground cinnamon
- 2 large eggs, separated
- 1 cup milk
- ½ cup canned pumpkin
- 2 tablespoons canola oil

1. In a large saucepan, combine the syrup ingredients. Bring to a boil over medium heat, stirring occasionally. Reduce heat; simmer, uncovered, for 20-25 minutes or until slightly thickened. Let stand for 30 minutes before serving.

2. For pancakes, in a large bowl, combine the dry ingredients. In another bowl, whisk the egg yolks, milk, pumpkin and oil until smooth. Stir into dry ingredients just until moistened. In a small bowl, beat the egg whites until soft peaks form; fold into batter.

3. Pour batter by ¼ cupfuls onto a hot greased griddle. Turn when bubbles form on top of pancakes. Cook until second side is golden brown. Serve with syrup.

HELPFUL HINT

Apple cider is unfiltered juice that still contains the apple pulp and sediment. It's more perishable than apple juice, which is thoroughly filtered.

PUMPKIN SPICE CUPCAKES WITH CREAM CHEESE FROSTING

I love the flavor of pumpkin, especially during fall. Generously spiced with cinnamon, the cream cheese frosting in this recipe adds an extra-special touch.

—DEBBIE WIGGINS LONGMONT, CO

PREP: 25 MIN.
BAKE: 20 MIN. + COOLING
MAKES: 2 DOZEN

- ¾ **cup butter, softened**
- 2½ **cups sugar**
- 3 **large eggs**
- 1 **can (15 ounces) solid-pack pumpkin**
- 2⅓ **cups all-purpose flour**
- 1 **tablespoon pumpkin pie spice**
- 1 **teaspoon baking powder**
- 1 **teaspoon ground cinnamon**
- ¾ **teaspoon salt**
- ½ **teaspoon baking soda**
- ½ **teaspoon ground ginger**
- 1 **cup buttermilk**

FROSTING
- 1 **package (8 ounces) cream cheese, softened**
- ½ **cup butter, softened**
- 4 **cups confectioners' sugar**
- 1 **teaspoon vanilla extract**
- 2 **teaspoons ground cinnamon**

1. Preheat oven to 350°. In a large bowl, cream butter and sugar until light and fluffy. Add eggs, one at a time, beating well after each addition. Add pumpkin. Combine flour, pie spice, baking powder, cinnamon, salt, baking soda and ginger; add to creamed mixture alternately with buttermilk, beating well after each addition.

2. Fill 24 paper-lined muffin cups three-fourths full. Bake for 20-25 minutes or until a toothpick inserted in the center comes out clean. Cool 10 minutes before removing from pans to wire racks to cool completely.

3. For frosting, in a large bowl, beat the cream cheese and butter until fluffy. Add confectioners' sugar, vanilla and cinnamon; beat until smooth. Frost cupcakes. Refrigerate the leftovers.

HELPFUL HINT

Instead of buying buttermilk, you can place 1 tablespoon white vinegar or lemon juice in a liquid measuring cup and add enough milk to measure 1 cup. Stir, then let stand for 5 minutes. Or you can substitute 1 cup plain yogurt for the buttermilk.

PUMPKIN & CAULIFLOWER GARLIC MASH

START TO FINISH: 25 MIN.
MAKES: 6 SERVINGS

- 1 medium head cauliflower, broken into florets (about 6 cups)
- 3 garlic cloves
- ⅓ cup spreadable cream cheese
- 1 can (15 ounces) solid-pack pumpkin
- 1 tablespoon minced fresh thyme
- 1 teaspoon salt
- ¼ teaspoon cayenne pepper
- ¼ teaspoon pepper

1. Place 1 in. of water in a large saucepan; bring to a boil. Add cauliflower and garlic cloves; cook, covered, 8-10 minutes or until tender. Drain; transfer to a food processor.

2. Add remaining ingredients; process until smooth. Return to pan; heat through, stirring occasionally.

I wanted healthy alternatives to my family's favorite recipes. Pumpkin, cauliflower and thyme make an amazing dish. You'll never miss those plain old mashed potatoes.

—KARI WHEATON SOUTH BELOIT, IL

BONUS: DAY OF THE DEAD

DAY OF THE DEAD COOKIES

I make these almond butter cookies for all occasions. In spring, I cut them in flower shapes and insert a lollipop stick in each, then make a bouquet. Using candies, food coloring and a wild imagination, try your hand at this Mexican-Halloween inspired version.

—KRISSY FOSSMEYER HUNTLEY, IL

PREP: 2 HOURS + CHILLING
BAKE: 10 MIN./BATCH + COOLING
MAKES: 1 DOZEN

- 1¼ **cups butter, softened**
- 1¾ **cups confectioners' sugar**
- 2 **ounces almond paste**
- 1 **large egg**
- ¼ **cup 2% milk**
- 1 **teaspoon vanilla extract**
- 4 **cups all-purpose flour**
- ½ **teaspoon salt**
- 2 **packages (12 ounces each) white candy coating melts**
   Decorations of your choice:
     jumbo sprinkles, peppermint candies, candy-coated sunflower kernels, Skittles, Twizzlers Rainbow Twists and Good & Plenty candies
   Black paste food coloring

1. In a large bowl, cream butter and confectioners' sugar until light and fluffy; add almond paste. Beat in the egg, milk and vanilla. Combine flour and salt; gradually add to creamed mixture and mix well. Cover and refrigerate for 1 hour.

2. On a lightly floured surface, roll out dough to ¼-in. thickness. Cut out with a floured 5-in. skull-shaped cookie cutter. Place 1 in. apart on ungreased baking sheets.

3. Bake at 375° for 7-9 minutes or until firm. Let stand for 2 minutes before removing to wire racks to cool completely.

4. In a large, shallow microwave-safe dish, melt white candy melts according to package directions. Dip top side of each cookie into coating, allowing excess to drip off; place on waxed paper.

5. Add decorations as desired. Tint remaining white coating black; pipe on mouth. Let stand until set.

NOTE *The skull cookie cutter is available from Copper Gifts at their website* (coppergifts.com), *or call 1-620-421-0654.*

QUICK BLACK BEAN QUESADILLAS

Back when our youngsters were in grade school, I copied this recipe from an old Mexican cookbook to serve at a classroom party. Since then, we've made it at home many times. It's an easy dinner for you to pull together when time is short.

—DIXIE TERRY GOREVILLE, IL

START TO FINISH: 25 MIN.
MAKES: 4 SERVINGS

- 1 **cup canned black beans, rinsed and drained**
- 1 **green onion, chopped**
- 2 **tablespoons chopped red onion**
- 2 **tablespoons finely chopped roasted sweet red pepper**
- 1 **tablespoon minced fresh cilantro**
- 1 **tablespoon lime juice**
- 1 **garlic clove, minced**
- 4 **flour tortillas (10 inches)**
- 1 **cup shredded Muenster or Monterey Jack cheese**

1. In a small bowl, mash beans with a fork; stir in the green onion, red onion, pepper, cilantro, lime juice and garlic. Spread ¼ cup bean mixture over half of each tortilla; top with ¼ cup cheese. Fold over.

2. Cook on a griddle coated with cooking spray over low heat for 1-2 minutes on each side or until cheese is melted. Cut into wedges.

HORCHATA

The mixture of ground rice and almonds is accented with a hint of lime in this popular drink. Depending on your preference, you can use more or less water for a thinner or creamier beverage. Either way, it's delicious.

—JAMES SCHEND PLEASANT PRAIRIE, WI

PREP: 5 MIN. + STANDING • **PROCESS:** 10 MIN.
MAKES: 6 SERVINGS

- ¾ **cup uncooked long grain rice**
- 2 **cups blanched almonds**
- 1 **cinnamon stick (3 inches)**
- 1½ **teaspoons grated lime peel**
- 4 **cups hot water**
- 1 **cup sugar**
- 1 **cup cold water**
  Ground cinnamon, optional
  Lime wedges, optional

1. Place rice in a blender; cover and process 2-3 minutes or until very fine. Transfer to a large bowl; add almonds, cinnamon stick, lime peel and hot water. Let stand, covered, at room temperature 8 hours.

2. Discard cinnamon stick. Transfer rice mixture to a blender; cover and process 3-4 minutes or until smooth. Add sugar; process until sugar is dissolved.

3. Place a strainer over a pitcher; line with double-layered cheesecloth. Pour rice mixture over cheesecloth; using a ladle, press mixture through strainer.

4. Stir in cold water. Serve over ice. If desired, sprinkle with cinnamon and serve with lime wedges.

TEQUILA-LIME FRUIT SALAD

START TO FINISH: 20 MIN.
MAKES: 10 SERVINGS

- ¾ **cup sugar**
- ¼ **cup water**
- ¼ **cup lime juice**
- 3 **tablespoons tequila or additional lime juice**
- 2 **cups cubed fresh pineapple**
- 2 **cups sliced fresh strawberries**
- 2 **cups chopped peeled kiwifruit**
- 2 **cups seedless red grapes, halved**

1. In a small saucepan, bring sugar and water to a boil over medium heat. Remove from the heat; cool completely. Stir in lime juice and tequila.

2. In a large bowl, combine the fruit. Drizzle with the syrup and toss gently to coat.

Looking for a fast, colorful side to round out any meal? This refreshing fruit salad is pure perfection!

—ANGELA HOWLAND HAYNESVILLE, ME

HELPFUL HINT

Tequila comes in two main types: gold (amber-colored) and silver (clear). Gold tequila may be aged or have caramel coloring or flavoring added to mimic the aging process. Silver tequila has a crisper, brighter taste, and you may prefer it in this salad.

COFFIN PUMPKIN CAKE

The maple flavoring in the frosting makes this spooky spice cake delicious! And the gingersnap crumbs make the coffin look like a pine box—it suits this season perfectly.

—KATHY MICHEL DUBUQUE, IA

PREP: 1 HOUR
BAKE: 40 MIN. + COOLING
MAKES: 20 SERVINGS

- ¾ cup butter, softened
- 1½ cups sugar
- 3 large eggs
- 1½ cups canned pumpkin
- 1½ teaspoons vanilla extract
- 3 cups all-purpose flour
- 1½ teaspoons ground cinnamon
- 1 teaspoon baking powder
- 1 teaspoon baking soda
- ¾ teaspoon ground nutmeg
- ½ teaspoon salt
- ¼ teaspoon ground ginger
- ¼ teaspoon ground cloves
- 1 cup buttermilk

FROSTING/FILLING

- 2 packages (8 ounces each) cream cheese, softened
- ½ cup butter, softened
- 3½ cups confectioners' sugar
- 2 to 3 teaspoons maple flavoring
- ½ cup heavy whipping cream
- 2 cups crushed gingersnap cookies (about 40 cookies)

1. In a large bowl, cream butter and sugar until light and fluffy. Add eggs, one at a time, beating well after each addition. Beat in the pumpkin and vanilla. Combine flour, cinnamon, baking powder, baking soda, nutmeg, salt, ginger and cloves; add to pumpkin mixture alternately with buttermilk, beating well after each addition.

2. Line a greased 13x9-in. baking pan with waxed paper and grease the paper; spread batter into pan. Bake at 325° for 40-45 minutes or until a toothpick inserted in the center comes out clean. Cool for 5 minutes before removing from pan to a wire rack to cool completely.

3. In a large bowl, beat cream cheese and butter until smooth. Add the confectioners' sugar and enough maple flavoring to achieve a spreading consistency. For the filling, in a small bowl, beat 1 cup frosting with whipping cream until soft peaks form.

4. Cut cake into a coffin shape (discard scraps or save for another use). Cut cake horizontally into two layers. Place the bottom layer on a serving plate; spread with filling. Top with second layer.

5. Set aside 2 tablespoons frosting for writing; frost cake with the remaining frosting. Sprinkle with cookie crumbs. Cut a small hole in the corner of a plastic bag; fill with reserved frosting. Pipe RIP onto cake. Store in the refrigerator.

MINI CHICKEN EMPANADAS

Refrigerated pie crust makes quick work of assembling these bite-sized appetizers loaded with chicken and cheese. A friend passed along this recipe to me, and it's become one of my favorites for finger food at parties.

—**BETTY FULKS** ONIA, AR

PREP: 30 MIN. • **BAKE:** 15 MIN./BATCH
MAKES: ABOUT 2½ DOZEN

- 1 **cup finely chopped cooked chicken**
- ⅔ **cup shredded Colby-Monterey Jack cheese**
- 3 **tablespoons cream cheese, softened**
- 4 **teaspoons chopped sweet red pepper**
- 2 **teaspoons chopped seeded jalapeno pepper**
- 1 **teaspoon ground cumin**
- ½ **teaspoon salt**
- ⅛ **teaspoon pepper**
- 1 **package (14.1 ounces) refrigerated pie crusts**

1. In a small bowl, combine the first eight ingredients. On a lightly floured surface, roll each pie crust sheet into a 15-inch circle. Cut with a floured 3-in. round biscuit cutter.

2. Place about 1 teaspoon filling on one half of each circle. Moisten edges with water. Fold crust over filling. Press edges with a fork to seal.

3. Transfer to greased baking sheets. Bake at 400° for 12-15 minutes or until golden brown. Remove to wire racks. Serve warm.

NOTE *Wear disposable gloves when cutting hot peppers; the oils can burn skin. Avoid touching your face.*

MEXICAN HOT CHOCOLATE

START TO FINISH: 10 MIN.
MAKES: 4 SERVINGS

- ¼ **cup baking cocoa**
- 2 **tablespoons brown sugar**
- 1 **cup boiling water**
- ¼ **teaspoon ground cinnamon**
  Dash ground cloves or nutmeg
- 3 **cups milk**
- 1 **teaspoon vanilla extract**
  Whipped cream
  Whole cinnamon sticks

1. In a small saucepan, mix cocoa and sugar; stir in water. Bring to a boil. Reduce heat; cook for 2 minutes, stirring mixture constantly.

2. Add cinnamon and cloves; stir in the milk. Simmer for 5 minutes (do not boil). Whisk in the vanilla. Pour the hot chocolate into mugs; top with whipped cream. Use whole cinnamon sticks for stirrers.

NOTE *To instantly give Mexican flair to hot cocoa from a mix, stir a little vanilla and ground cinnamon into the prepared cocoa. Garnish with canned whipped cream and a sprinkling of nutmeg if desired.*

This delicious, not-too-sweet hot chocolate is richly flavored with cocoa and delicately seasoned with spices. The blend of cinnamon and chocolate flavors is wonderful!

—KATHY YOUNG WEATHERFORD, TX

CHICKEN TAMALES

I love tamales. They take a little time to make but are so worth the effort, and for us, a must at family get-togethers.
—**CINDY PRUITT** GROVE, OK

PREP: 2½ HOURS + SOAKING
COOK: 50 MIN.
MAKES: 20 TAMALES

- 24 **dried corn husks**
- 1 **broiler/fryer chicken (3 to 4 pounds), cut up**
- 1 **medium onion, quartered**
- 2 **teaspoons salt**
- 1 **garlic clove, crushed**
- 3 **quarts water**

DOUGH
- 1 **cup shortening**
- 3 **cups masa harina**

FILLING
- 6 **tablespoons canola oil**
- 6 **tablespoons all-purpose flour**
- ¾ **cup chili powder**
- ½ **teaspoon salt**
- ¼ **teaspoon garlic powder**
- ¼ **teaspoon pepper**
- 2 **cans (2¼ ounces each) sliced ripe olives, drained**
  Hot water

1. Cover husks with cold water; soak until soft, at least 2 hours.
2. Place chicken, onion, salt and garlic in a 6-qt. stockpot. Pour in water; bring to a boil. Reduce heat; simmer, covered, until chicken is tender, 45-60 minutes. Remove chicken from broth. When cool enough to handle, remove bones and skin; discard. Shred chicken.

Strain cooking juices; skim the fat. Reserve 6 cups stock.
3. For dough, beat shortening until light and fluffy, about 1 minute. Beat in small amounts of masa harina alternately with small amounts of reserved stock, using no more than 2 cups stock. Drop a small amount of dough into a cup of cold water; dough should float. If not, continue beating, rechecking every minute.
4. For filling, heat oil in a Dutch oven; stir in flour until blended. Cook and stir over medium heat until lightly browned, 7-9 minutes. Add the seasonings, chicken and remaining stock; bring to a boil. Reduce heat; simmer, uncovered, stirring occasionally, until thickened, about 45 minutes.
5. Drain husks and pat dry; tear four husks to make 20 strips for tying tamales. (To prevent husks from drying out, cover with plastic wrap and a damp towel until ready to use.) On the wide end of each remaining corn husk, spread 3 tablespoons dough to within ½ in. of sides; top each with 2 tablespoons chicken filling and 2 teaspoons olives. Fold long sides of husk over filling, overlapping slightly. Fold over narrow end of husk; tie with a strip of husk to secure.
6. Place a large steamer basket in the stockpot over water; place tamales upright in steamer. Bring to a boil; steam, covered, adding hot water as needed, until dough peels away from husk, about 45 minutes.

TURKEY POSOLE

This soup is a favorite because it makes good use of leftover roasted turkey. And it's quick, easy and tasty. No one feels like they're eating leftovers because this soup tastes nothing like traditional turkey with gravy.

—MARGEE BERRY WHITE SALMON, WA

START TO FINISH: 30 MIN.
MAKES: 6 SERVINGS

- 2 cans (14½ ounces each) reduced-sodium chicken broth
- 1 jar (16 ounces) chunky salsa
- 1 can (15 ounces) hominy, rinsed and drained
- 2 teaspoons chipotle hot pepper sauce
- ½ teaspoon ground cumin
- 2 cups cubed cooked turkey breast
- ¼ cup sour cream
- ⅓ cup shredded cheddar or Monterey Jack cheese
- ⅓ cup minced fresh cilantro
- ⅓ cup crushed blue tortilla chips
- ¼ cup shredded red or green cabbage

In a large saucepan, combine the first five ingredients. Bring to a boil; reduce heat. Simmer, uncovered, for 10 minutes. Stir in turkey; heat through. Top servings with sour cream, cheese, cilantro, chips and cabbage.

NOTES

TRES LECHES CUPCAKES

A sweet silky mixture using a trio of milks makes these little cakes three times as good. Because they soak overnight, they're a great make-ahead dessert for a potluck.

—TASTE OF HOME TEST KITCHEN

PREP: 45 MIN. + CHILLING
BAKE: 15 MIN. + COOLING
MAKES: 4 DOZEN

- 1 **package yellow cake mix (regular size)**
- 1¼ **cups water**
- 4 **large eggs**
- 1 **can (14 ounces) sweetened condensed milk**
- 1 **cup coconut milk**
- 1 **can (5 ounces) evaporated milk**
  Dash salt

WHIPPED CREAM

- 3 **cups heavy whipping cream**
- ⅓ **cup confectioners' sugar**
  Assorted fresh berries

1. Preheat the oven to 350°. Line 48 muffin cups with paper liners.

2. In a large bowl, combine cake mix, water and eggs; beat on low speed 30 seconds. Beat on medium 2 minutes.

3. Fill prepared cups halfway, allowing room in liners for milk mixture. Bake for 11-13 minutes or until a toothpick inserted in center comes out clean. Cool 5 minutes before removing from pans to wire racks; cool slightly.

4. Place the cupcakes in 15x10x1-in. pans. Poke holes in cupcakes with a skewer. In a small bowl, mix milks and salt; spoon scant 1 tablespoon mixture over each cupcake. Refrigerate, covered, overnight.

5. In a large bowl, beat cream until it begins to thicken. Add confectioners' sugar; beat until soft peaks form. Spread over cupcakes; top with berries. Store cupcakes in the refrigerator.

HELPFUL HINT

To make this sangria punch
with alcohol, substitute a
bottle of chilled sparkling
wine for the ginger ale
and omit the club soda.

SANGRIA MOCKTAIL

Everyone can join in the toast with this light and refreshing drink. It tastes just like champagne, complete with bubbles!

—PAM ION GAITHERSBURG, MD

PREP: 10 MIN. + FREEZING
MAKES: 8 SERVINGS

- 3 **cups white grape juice, divided**
- 2 **cans (12 ounces each) ginger ale, chilled**
- ½ **cup chilled club soda**
  Orange slices and sliced fresh strawberries

1. Pour 2 cups juice into ice cube trays; freeze until set.
2. Transfer ice cubes to a pitcher; add remaining juice. Slowly stir in ginger ale and club soda. Garnish with oranges and strawberries. Serve punch immediately.

NOTES

RECIPE INDEX